I'm Not a Terrorist,
but I've Played One on TV

Memoirs of a Middle Eastern Funny Man

Maz Jobrani

Simon & Schuster Paperbacks

New York   London   Toronto   Sydney   New Delhi

Simon & Schuster Paperbacks
An Imprint of Simon & Schuster, Inc.
1230 Avenue of the Americas
New York, NY 10020

First Simon & Schuster paperback edition February 2016

SIMON & SCHUSTER PAPERBACKS and colophon are
registered trademarks of Simon & Schuster, Inc.

For information about special discounts for bulk purchases,
please contact Simon & Schuster Special Sales
at 1-866-506-1949 or business@simonandschuster.com.

The Simon & Schuster Speakers Bureau can bring authors to your live event.
For more information or to book an event contact the
Simon & Schuster Speakers Bureau at 1-866-248-3049
or visit our website at www.simonspeakers.com.

Interior design by Ruth Lee-Mui
Jacket design by Jonathan Bush
Jacket photograph by Paul Mobley Photography
Digital art by Mike Campau

Manufactured in the United States of America

1   3   5   7   9   10   8   6   4   2

The Library of Congress has cataloged the hardcover edition as follows:

Jobrani, Maziyar, date.
I'm not a terrorist, but I've played one on tv : memoirs of a
Middle Eastern funny man / Maz Jobrani.
pages cm
1. Jobrani, Maziyar. Comedians—United States—Biography.
3. Actors—United States—Biography. 4. Iranian Americans—Biography.
5. Stereotypes (Social psychology)—United States. I. Title.
PN2287.J573A3 2014
792.702'8092—dc23
[B]
2014015012

ISBN 978-1-4767-4998-3
ISBN 978-1-14767-4999-0 (pbk)
ISBN 978-1-4767-5000-2 (ebook)

*Dedicated to Joe Rein,
the man who reminded me to
pursue my dream*

Contents

Introduction

Hello there! Thank you for picking up my book. Maybe you picked it up because you recognize me from a television show. "Isn't that the guy from *Better Off Ted* and *Knights of Prosperity* and *Life on a Stick*? Whatever happened to those shows? What happens to actors when their shows get canceled?"

Well, reader, we write books. That's what happens when our shows get canceled. Maybe you've picked up this book because you saw the word "terrorist" on the cover and thought: *I always knew this guy was a terrorist! Always trying to convince the American public that he's a stand-up comedian. What a dirty piece of scum! He was never that funny anyway!* Or maybe you're related to me, and you thought: *What the hell—Maz wrote a book? I wonder if he mentions me. I better buy a copy and check it out.*

Whatever the reason, thank you.

Writing a book isn't easy. I'm a comedian, so I'm used to

writing a few lines of comedy each day, but when I was faced with writing two hundred pages I was intimidated. I immediately began to think of ways to cheat. What if I double-spaced everything? Or maybe I could add a hundred pages of pictures. That would really help move this baby along.

However, once I began writing, it started to flow. After all, this is a story about my life. Who's more qualified to write about me than *me*? I've been studying me for forty-two years. I'm an expert on me. I've got a Ph.D. in me. I wrote the book on me. Literally! And what a life it's been! A classic immigrant story. A kid from the streets of Tehran moving to the streets of Los Angeles. (Which nowadays is packed with so many Iranians that it's basically like living back on the streets of Tehran.) Along the way I've experienced a revolution, a hostage crisis, and male-pattern baldness.

Writing a book is like going through a therapy session. It's amazing how much you forget about your past until you're forced to sit at a desk and put it down on paper. If you want to go through therapy but can't afford the payments, try writing a book. When you've got a busy life filled with work, family, car payments, Twitter feeds, and Facebook photos, you don't have as much time to reflect on your past. But when you have an editor with deadlines, you're forced to dig, and you find that you have stories to tell. Like the one about how I was made to wear a turban on a Chuck Norris movie of the week. Yes, I know, you're jealous. Don't hate—we can't all be friends (or, in my case, enemies) with Chuck.

In imitation of the therapeutic process, I tell my story as I remember it. Some of the dialogue you will read wasn't said word for word but what it actually sounded like when I heard it. My mother, whom you will read a lot about in this book, is a prime example. Anyone who has reflected on a parental relationship knows that when a mother says one thing, her kid can read a million other things into it. For example, when my mom would say, "Why can't you go to medical school like Mina's son?" I would hear "You're a bum loser, and you're a disgrace to our entire race! I never should have had you in the first place!" In fairness to my mom, she was no Joan Crawford from *Mommie Dearest*. She was always a loving mother who did what she thought was best. Sometimes that included hitting us with clothes hangers when we were young, but I'm sure we had it coming. To this day I have flashbacks when the dry cleaner asks me if I want my shirts folded or on hangers. I love my mom dearly, and thanks to her all my shirts now come home from the dry cleaner's folded.

Since my life as a comedian involves so much traveling, you could call this a travel book as well. You will read about my experiences in bars in Lebanon with Christian Lebanese (yes, there's alcohol in the Middle East, and Christians, too!). You will read about my visit to one of the Wonders of the World, Petra in Jordan, where not only did I see the historical city built thousands of years ago, but I was peddled *Indiana Jones* merchandise. American capitalism at its best! There's also my trip to the White House, where President Obama groped my wife. You want scandal? I've got scandal! The point is, I've traveled a lot. You know you're flying too much when you consistently hit more than a hundred thousand miles per year. I've gotten to know the shuttle bus drivers at the parking lot, the flight attendants, and even some sure-handed TSA agents. In fact, just the other day a TSA agent fist-bumped me as I went through the metal detector—that's how close we've become. Since I'm of Middle Eastern descent, the first time a TSA agent recognized me I was worried she was profiling me. Turns out she was a fan of my stand-up and just wanted to

Part One

Fighting Chuck Norris and Stereotypes, in That Order

Dallas, Texas

I was born in Iran and grew up in America. That makes me a Middle Eastern American. The only thing more intimidating for a Middle Eastern guy than going to Texas is going to Texas to meet Chuck Norris. Talk about the official Heartland of America. When it comes to terrorists, Chuck has a 100 percent kill rate, usually televised at two o'clock in the morning. One of my first big breaks was to star as a terrorist in that Chuck Norris movie I mentioned in the Introduction. Yes, I was blessed with greatness early on. So off I went to Dallas to meet him.

Most of what I knew about Dallas I learned from stereotypes picked up in my childhood. When I first came to America in the late 1970s, I didn't know much about American sports. I was only six at the time and had played soccer back in Iran. I had never heard of American football. So once I began to settle in I started to learn how this foreign game was played.

"I get the part at the beginning where the guy kicks the ball. Why does the other guy catch it? Is he the goalkeeper? Why is he being chased by all the other guys? Does he owe them money? Why is everyone dressed in tights? These are the biggest and meanest ballerinas I've ever seen. Why are they hitting each other so hard? Do they have anger issues? I know why they're angry. Because their ball isn't round. Balls are supposed to be round. Who makes an oblong ball? You have no idea which way it's going to bounce. I'd be pissed, too! Whoa, whoa, whoa—who are the girls dancing on the sidelines? How do they fit in? You mean they get paid just to cheer? What a country!"

Once these concerns had been properly addressed, my friend Sam—another Iranian kid who'd been in the United States for a while—led me to my first favorite sports team: the Dallas Cowboys. This was the late seventies, so the best teams in the NFL were the Dallas Cowboys and the Pittsburgh Steelers. Unaware of what the Cowboys stood for, I became a fan and only later found out that I was rooting for what was known then as "America's Team." *What better way to become an American*, I thought, *than to be a fan of the most Americanny American of teams that ever existed. Plus, they have hot cheerleaders!*

In recent years, the Cowboys have fallen from this pedestal as they have been afflicted with drug, sex, and violence scandals—which would be okay if they were winning. (Doing coke with a hooker in a motel and shooting people makes you un-American if the squad cannot maintain a winning record and make the playoffs at least every other year.) At any rate, when I was a kid, loving the Cowboys was like loving John Wayne and hot dogs. It made you American even if your papers said you were an alien—a legal alien, but an alien nonetheless. The Cowboys became my first exposure to what I thought represented the heartland of the country.

Iranians Love Soaps

As a result, I became fascinated with Texas, specifically the city of Dallas. My next exposure to the American Southwest came in the form of the television show *Dallas*, which the women in my family watched every week. Back in Iran, American film and TV were huge. My grandmother had a crush on the Six Million Dollar Man and she knew I loved him, too. She would tell me all the time that he had come over the night before and that I had fallen asleep just before he got there. She called him her "friend."

"My ferend vas here last night just after you fall asleep."

"Which friend?"

"Eh-Steve Austin." Iranians cannot pronounce words that have back-to-back consonants. So Steve becomes Eh-Steve, traffic becomes te-raffic, gangster becomes gang-ester, and so forth. We also pronounce w's as v's. Thus my grandmother would say "ve" instead of "we."

"You mean the Six Million Dollar Man?"

"Yes, I call him Eh-Steve. Ve are on the first name basis."

"Did you at least take a picture with him?"

"He's too fast! He make dat sound and run avay before I get chance. Na-na-na-na-na-na! Next time."

All the women in my family were obsessed with American television. From *Dallas* to *Dynasty*, we followed these characters' lives closely until they became our extended family. As a result, one thing that escaped my parents was the idea of what might be appropriate for a kid to watch. If they were watching the Ewings on *Dallas* or the Carringtons on *Dynasty* they never thought: *Is all this sex and scandal okay for an eight-year-old to watch?*

Whereas my American friends' parents might not let them

watch *Dallas* because of its mature themes and late time slot, my parents didn't care. I don't think immigrant parents really understand the ratings system. They think that PG (Parental Guidance) means that a movie will give "parental guidance" to your kid while you go shopping for gold jewelry, chandeliers, and marble counters at the mall. So you can drop them off for a few hours and they will watch the movie while the movie is watching them. I even remember my aunt turning on *The Exorcist* and not thinking twice while we sat next to her as Linda Blair's head did a 360 and puked out green vomit. Who lets their eight-year-old watch *The Exorcist*? It's possible they misunderstood and thought the movie was about exercising. When they saw my prepubescent face, all contorted and scared, they developed a callous attitude: "Look at this lazy child of ours. You are big pussy! You are afraid of exercising? You need to vatch that movie again. You're looking a bit chubby."

Every week the women in my family would follow the soap opera revolving around the Ewings and their oil empire. I don't know what drew my family to the Ewings, but I suppose our affluence and coming from a country rich in oil might have had something to do with it. Once *Dallas* got old they started watching *Dynasty*—more rich people surrounded by scandal.

My grandmother didn't speak much English, but she religiously watched and understood all these soap operas better than the rest of us. Sometimes when I was home sick from school, she would take care of me and turn on *General Hospital* and tell me all the details of every story line.

"Dat guy married to dat girl, but she doesn't know he not really deh guy, but his evil tvin. Deh real guy kept hostage in basement vhile the evil tvin try to get all of de money ferom deh girl.

Dat von der is deh girl's fader who is a really good guy and a philanthropist. Ve like him, Maz."

"How do you get all that?"

"Because I'm not idiot."

"But you barely speak English."

"Yes, but I understand love. I understand dese people. Ve are the same."

I would watch these shows and I even became such a Joan Collins fan that I read one of her sister's books. How an eight-year-old Iranian boy from Marin County got his hands on a Jackie Collins book is a mystery. My parents could barely read the back of a toothpaste tube in English, much less a whole novel. I think one of my aunts or my older sister had picked it up so I decided to give it a read, which made me yearn to be older immediately. I remember thinking, *Wow! Adults have so much sex and scandal and money! I can't wait to grow up!*

Buying Dog Food for a Stripper

The Ewings and the Cowboys, Joan Collins and her literary sister—these were the people I thought of when I thought of Texas. My first time going to Dallas was to do the Chuck Norris movie, and I remember asking some of the locals how things worked.

"Where do people go out in Dallas? What's the thing to do at night?"

"Strip clubs."

"Okay, but where do the locals go out? Where do J. R. and Bobby Ewing hang out?"

"You mean Larry Hagman and Patrick Duffy?"

"Sure, I guess."

"They're actors. They probably hang out in Los Angeles somewhere."

"I just came from Los Angeles."

"Maybe you'll see them when you go back."

"I guess I'll go to a strip club then. Just to see if they're hanging out there."

Quickly my glamorous image of Dallas dissipated and reality set in. Don't get me wrong, there's a lot of cultural stuff to do in Dallas—like going to the Book Depository where Lee Harvey shot JFK. However, when you ask local dudes what a dude from Los Angeles should do to experience authentic Dallas nightlife, four out of five will tell you to go to a strip club.

Middle Eastern men are stereotypically known to be macho—IROC-Z, gold chain, Drakkar Noir, manly men. (Basically like Italians, but using words that have the KHHHHH sound.) Some of these men might still exist with multiple wives they don't talk to, kids they don't play catch with, and girlfriends they take to clubs for bottle service. However, in this modern age where women have stepped up to run companies and men have been encouraged to talk to therapists about their feelings, most of the Middle Eastern men I know no longer fit the stereotype. My Middle Eastern friends change diapers, ask permission of their wives to watch a football game with friends, and shuttle kids around in SUVs. And in keeping with the image of the modern Middle Eastern male, I'm going to come right out and say it: I HATE STRIP CLUBS! I know some of the old-school macho Middle Eastern men are dropping this book right now saying, "Okay, dats it. I've had enough! Vhat kind of fancy pansy bullshit is dis? KHHHH-HHH." I'm sorry to say, it's the truth.

I know some men love strip clubs, and even the nineteen

hijackers from September 11 were reported to have gone to some on the nights before they attacked the World Trade Center and the Pentagon. As if I didn't hate these guys enough, hearing that they went to strip clubs gave me even more reason to despise them. Why would they go? I thought their ultimate goal was to obtain seventy-two virgins. I'm going out on a limb here, but my guess is there aren't a lot of virgins at strip clubs. And while we're on the topic of the seventy-two virgins as a motivation to kill yourself, which I have a tough time believing, my question is, why would these idiots want virgins in the first place? I've been with a few virgins in my life. It's not fun. I'm not too proud to admit it—I was once a virgin myself. I can tell you I had no idea what I was doing in my virgin days. So why someone would kill themselves to be with seventy-two inexperienced women is beyond me. You'd think they'd want someone who could show them a good time, expose them to questionable rashes, get them to swing on chandeliers, somersault onto the bed into perfect splits, slide down fireman's poles, that kind of stuff.

Before I ever went to a strip club, I always thought they'd be like Disneyland for adults. I thought you would enter to see the forbidden, experience sensuality, and revel in mystery. I soon came to realize that it was nothing like that, but more like a bus stop with naked women begging you for twenties. Which, by the way, would make taking the bus much more interesting. I think city officials should really consider hiring strippers to work bus stops—could help encourage public transportation. I'm just saying.

I know that some women reading this are rolling their eyes. "Yeah right, you don't like strip clubs. That's a bunch of crap." But I swear, there are a lot of men who feel uncomfortable in these places. Here's the best way I can explain it. There is a stereotype that women love shopping and the only thing they love more than shopping is shopping for shoes. Now, imagine trying on a bunch of beautiful, hot, sexy shoes but only having them spin around on your feet and then watching them go slip onto someone else's feet. You don't get to take them home; you don't get to keep them. You could, for another twenty bucks, try them on again, but there's a bouncer standing close by making sure you don't rub the shoes while you try them on. Yes, in this analogy there *are* shoe bouncers. Oh, and there's a two-drink minimum while you're trying on these shoes, even if you're not thirsty. As you can see, this could be really frustrating.

One of the tricks of strip clubs you figure out fast is that all of the songs are shortened. So whereas you might get a lap dance with a stripper on a song like Queen's "Bohemian Rhapsody," which is six minutes long, at a strip club it would last closer to two minutes. The song would finish and you'd turn to your friend:

"Was that six minutes? That didn't feel like six minutes."

"I don't know, bro, I'm drunk."

"We must be having so much fun that six minutes passed in two minutes. Let's get another dance."

"I'm with you, bro."

"Okay good—this next song is Pink Floyd's 'Shine on You Crazy Diamond,' which fortunately is seventeen minutes long. This is going to be a quality lap dance."

Two minutes later:

"Was that seventeen minutes? That didn't feel like seventeen minutes."

The other thing you experience is a false sense of your own attractiveness. All these hot young women are walking up to you asking if you want to hang out with them.

Wow, I think this new blazer I bought makes me look really hot because all of these scantily clad, beautiful women in lingerie keep staring at me. As Sally Field would say, "I can't deny the fact that you like me, right now, you like me!" Turns out that right then they just really liked my credit card, which at that time in my comic career was maxed out.

I once talked to a stripper for a while and the conversation came around to the fact that she needed a sugar daddy. She was telling me about her rent problems and how she had a little dog she needed to feed and the whole time I was thinking, *I wonder how many months' rent I could cover with my credit card that might have $250 left before it hits the limit. Maybe I could at least pay for a bag of dog food for her dog. I wonder if that gives me a shot with this girl.*

I know this is a story about Dallas, but to be completely honest the dog food conundrum occurred at a strip club in Los Angeles. There are so many Persians in Los Angeles and we have a reputation for being well-off financially, so perhaps this girl was thinking that I was a sheikh or a shah or at least a chiropractor—for some reason there's an inordinate number of Persian chiropractors in Los Angeles. I think it's because it's an easy way to consider yourself a doctor and impress people while also being able to charge insurance companies and make the kind of money to be able to afford a Mercedes-Benz, which every self-loving Persian owns—preferably in black with a personalized license plate like CHIRODK which could be read as Chiro Dick but is actually meant to be read as Chiro Doc.

But back to Dallas. My costar on the Chuck Norris film, who was also a Middle Easterner playing a terrorist, talked me into going to a strip club, since that seemed to be the place most recommended by the locals. At the time I was dating a girl who would later become my wife and I felt bad going to the strip club and not telling her even though I honestly didn't want to go. At some point I gave in to my guilt and decided to call her to tell her where I was.

"Honey, it's me. I have something very important to tell you."

"What?"

"I've just realized that I really, really love you."

"That's nice to hear, Maz. What made you come to this conclusion?"

"Well I'm at a strip club and I was talking to this stripper and I realized I had zero desire to get a lap dance from her. Then later, during the lap dance, the only person I was thinking about was you and I thought I'd call and let you know that I'm at a strip club and thinking about you."

"Where are you?"

"At a strip club. Even though a Jimi Hendrix song came on— and Jimi has something like a fifteen-minute blues riff in this one, which is one of the most efficient songs to get a lap dance to—I decided to call you instead."

Click.

"Honey? Hello? You don't like Jimi Hendrix?"

That was not the end of the stripper saga for my wife and me. Years later, my son Dhara came to a show at the Comedy Store in L.A. called *The Naughty Show.* I didn't think twice before taking him because I just had to stop in and do a set. It's like fifteen minutes, round-trip. As I'm waiting to go up they have a pole dancer come out and do a dance. I'm in the back getting ready to go on and not thinking at all that my four-year-old is out in the audience watching a stripper do a pole dance.

A few weeks later out of nowhere he mentions it. "Daddy, why was that lady dancing on a pole?"

I realized I had become my parents, letting my little

Iranian-Indian-American kid see things he was not supposed to see, like J. R. Ewing, and strippers.

"Um, she was actually an off-duty fireman. She was practicing going up and down the pole to save people."

I hope I didn't mess him up too bad. But mostly I hope he never tells my wife.

Fighting Chuck Norris

I was heading into this fantastic stripper and cowboy land to face down its favorite son in a battle for—well, a battle for the attention of television viewers awake at two o'clock in the morning on a Tuesday. This was before September 11, but even back then Hollywood supported the stereotype of Iranians and other Middle Easterners as members of an evil cabal. My earliest acting roles cast me in the way that I was, of course, paranoid that my fellow Americans saw me—as a terrorist. I was working then as an assistant at an advertising agency, and while I did not want to take these roles promoting a stereotype that I knew to be false, I felt I had to in order to build my career. I also wanted what most Americans wanted—to quit my day job. If that meant yelling "*Allah o akbar!*" at the climax of an action scene, right before the good guys killed me, so be it.

One of my early parts was in that movie starring Chuck Norris. As a Middle Eastern male, when you're in a Chuck Norris movie of the week you know you're going to die. You will never see a movie with Chuck and Hassan becoming besties and saving the world together.

"Hey Chuck—you get these guys and I'll get the other guys and see you back at the base. *Allah o akbar!*"

Those words will never be spoken in a Chuck Norris movie because audiences watch those movies to see Chuck Norris round-house kick anyone or anything that does not comply with Chuck Norris's worldview. They don't want Chuck Norris to get a Middle Eastern partner. They don't want Chuck Norris to be tolerant of other ethnicities and cultures. So when I got the call about auditioning for a Chuck Norris film, I knew it was for a bad guy.

The movie was titled—wait for it—*The President's Man: A Line in the Sand.* If you ever get the chance to watch this movie, don't. I played the role of a physicist who worked for an Osama bin Laden type who had come to Chicago to do what all Middle Eastern characters do in Chuck Norris films—attempt to blow up build-ings, then suffer a fury of Chuck Norris roundhouse kicks to the face. Again, this was *before* September 11.

I was torn. On the one hand, playing a terrorist and promoting this stereotype. On the other hand, quitting my day job. I found a compromise: I would bring humanity to the role and in the process move my career forward and be one step closer to quitting my day job. Maybe I could tweak my delivery of words such as, "I will kill you in the name of Allah!" What if I said those lines but made them more humane by posing them as a question? "I will kill you in the name of Allah?" "Would you mind if I killed you in the name of Allah?" "If I had to kill you in the name of anyone, is it okay to do so in the name of, oh, I don't know . . . Allah?" This Chuck Norris movie would be my ticket to stardom. Who knows, maybe I'd even win an Emmy for it. Actors have a little trick where we give characters backstory, imagining their lives before the pres-ent moment in order to more accurately tap into the persona. I decided I would bring depth to this character, really show the sophisticated American viewing public that watches movies at two o'clock in the morning on Tuesdays what made this guy tick. I dug deep to understand how my character had developed up until the point that Chuck Norris would kick him in the face—something along the lines of how he had been a kid in Afghanistan when the Russians attacked and killed his parents with arms supplied by the Great Satan, which furthered his hatred maybe not directly in regards to Chuck Norris, but Chuck Norris–related things, such as America. As you can see my logic was all twisted because if the Russians killed his parents, why would they use weapons from America? America was their enemy. None of this made sense.

I showed up at my wardrobe fitting feeling good about how I would portray this terrorist. Then the wardrobe lady handed me my outfit, which included a shirt, pants, and . . . a turban? Wait a second. I was playing an Afghan in America who wants to blow up a building. Afghans in America do not wear turbans. And Afghans in America planning to blow up buildings *definitely* do not wear turbans (unless they're hiding the bomb under the turban, in which case the turban could come in really handy).

"I've done my research," I begged the wardrobe lady. "I'm trying to bring humanity to this role. Don't you see? Russians killed his parents!"

She tilted her head, confused. "Then why does he want to kill Americans?"

"I don't know! Maybe he's just angry and wants to take it out on anyone. Or maybe he couldn't get a ticket to Moscow so he came to Chicago."

She shrugged. "Either way, this is the outfit the producers said to wear."

"But it doesn't make sense."

"And your story does?"

"Good point, but I still think he wouldn't wear the turban."

She shrugged again. "I'll let the producers know."

The next day when I showed up at my trailer, I looked in my closet to find a shirt, pants, and . . . a scarf.

"I see you spoke with the producers and they saw it my way. I appreciate that. And I will gladly wear this scarf instead. Thank you."

"That's not a scarf. That's the turban. You just gotta roll it up on your head."

"Are you kidding me? Did you even talk to the producers?"

"Yep! And they want you to wear the turban."

I spent the morning discussing it with anyone who would listen. "My character would want to blend in." "The turban is so cliché." "He had a rough childhood." "He's just misunderstood, really." "He'd rather be in Moscow!" Everyone nodded, but they were all in cahoots and certain that the turban was cinematic gold.

Come to find out, everyone who works on a Chuck Norris film is somehow related to Chuck Norris. The director was Chuck's kid. The executive producer was Chuck's brother. All of the Norrises had decided—probably at Norris Sunday supper over giant bowls of meat—that the bad guy would be easier for the audience to recognize at two o'clock on a Tuesday morning if he was wearing a turban.

Worse than furious, I was humiliated. Why did I think I could bring humanity to this character? It was a Chuck Norris movie, after all. Adding insult to injury, it was a Chuck Norris movie in which Chuck Norris played a college professor. But I was still looking forward to the fight scene between Chuck and me, a moment that I hoped would become iconic in the Norris oeuvre.

On the day we were set to shoot the fight scene, Norris showed up and had a word with his son. Why this never came up when all the Norrises had gathered around to craft this masterpiece in the first place we'll never know, but Chuck decided rather than fighting me, it would be much easier just to shoot me. In my head I had choreographed this amazing fight scene where Chuck and I would go blow for blow, then he would eventually pull on my turban and it would unravel, making me spin and get dizzy. Chuck would give my character the final roundhouse kick to the face, and I would be immortalized on film. Instead, he just had me run toward him with a machine gun in my hand and he took out a pistol and shot me. Nice and quick. No time to milk it. Good-bye Emmy!

By the time the film was ready, September 11 had occurred. I was mortified that they might release it but fairly certain they would not. Then, a couple months after 9/11, I read that Chuck Norris had actually come out and pushed to release the movie, claiming it was a patriotic film because the terrorists got what they deserved. I was worried people would see me in the streets and think I was an actual terrorist: "Hey, ain't that the sumbitch hassling Chuck Norris the other night on channel eight? Let's get him!"

I wrote letters to Chuck and CBS, asking them to *not* run the movie, but I heard nothing back. Soon I saw it on my TV listings and steeled myself to watch. The good news was that it was so, so bad, I couldn't get past the first ten minutes. I found reason to hope that very few people would be able to bear watching long enough to get to my scenes. I thought to myself, *Someone should shoot me not for being a terrorist, but for agreeing to do this movie.*

Lights, Camera, You Go!

After that I told my agents no more terrorist parts, no matter what. After all, 99.99 percent of Middle Eastern people are *not* terrorists, and by playing one on television I was promoting this stereotype. So I said, "That's it, never again." Then the show *24* called. They said they had a part for a terrorist.

"No!" I told them.

"But," they continued, "he changes his mind halfway through the mission!"

"Ahhh, the ambivalent terrorist! I suppose it doesn't hurt to play just ONE more," I said. "I mean, this guy's a terrorist with a heart of gold. I'll bring humanity to the role. And then quit my day job. Emmy Awards, take two."

Even my family and friends were getting tired of watching me die. It's exhausting bragging to people that you were hired to star in a movie or show and alerting them to when the program will air, all the while knowing that the story will climax with your death. After the episode of *24* aired, my mother called to discuss my burgeoning film career.

"Vhy you keep dying?"

"What do you mean why do I keep dying? This is the movies. That's how they write it, Mom."

"Vhy don't you kill *dem* von time?"

"I can't just kill them. There are scripts, wardrobes, directors, other actors. I can't just start doing my own thing."

"Sure you can. Vhen they say 'lights, camera,' you go on camera. Don't vait for 'action,' you little pussy. That movie you were in vith Chuck Norris—I vatch again the other day. There vas plenty of opportunities to kill him, but he kill you instead."

It was not just me who was sick of dying. It was my mother, too. And that's when I took my final stand and stopped taking these parts. I have not played or auditioned for another terrorist role in more than ten years. My management knew about my choice and although they supported it, there were times they just wanted to triple-check that I was still standing strong.

One time my agent called and said, "I'm about to pass on an audition for a big film for you but just wanted to make sure you're cool with it."

"What's the audition?"

"Three words—United. Ninety. Three."

"It's about the flight on nine-eleven?"

"Yep."

"Any good guys?"

"Yeah, but they're all white."

"I guess it's a pass."

Sometimes I'd see the advertisements for these films—big billboards posted around Los Angeles—and think, *Am I shooting myself in the foot?* But then the films would come out and I would spend my hard-earned American money to see them and remember how uncomfortable I would have felt portraying an Arab terrorist. Especially after the good feeling I had when I took a stand all those years ago. So I haven't worked in ten years, but at least I feel good about myself.

Okay, truth be told, I *have* worked. I've played cab drivers, donut shop owners, falafel stand cooks, and even doctors. Yes, an actual doctor. One who didn't try to hijack the hospital. Hey, don't judge—breaking stereotypes takes time.

Years ago I ended up on the *Colbert Report,* where my position on the matter came up during our interview.

"You refuse to audition for a part of a terrorist?" Stephen Colbert asked.

"That's right."

"Well, I agree. That's insulting," he said. "At this point in your career you should be *offered* the role of a terrorist."

"I'd rather just not do them."

"Why not?"

"The reason is, being of Middle Eastern descent, I feel there's more to Middle Eastern people, and you can see terrorism on the news all the time."

"But someone has to play the terrorists out there. We need the terrorist figure in movies to focus our rage."

"But you can focus your rage at the news that shows the terrorists," I said.

"Then who should play the terrorist? Would you want to see white actors in Arab face?"

"Or Latinos," I suggested. "They kind of look Middle Eastern."

"They could pass," Colbert agreed. "They could pass."

A couple years later I got the part of an Arab-American Secret Service agent in the movie *The Interpreter*, with Nicole Kidman and Sean Penn. This was a big win for me because I thought I had no chance in hell of getting the part. I auditioned for Sydney Pollack on tape, which means that you don't even go into an audition room. You just film yourself and mail it in. Even when they called me and told me I had the part I thought that maybe they had picked another guy and gotten me mixed up with him. I know this happens with other minorities where people say all Asians look alike or all black people look alike, so why not with Middle Easterners? It's even happened to me in the past where people have confused me with my fellow Middle Eastern–American comedian Ahmed Ahmed, who is Egyptian and looks nothing like me (meaning he has hair and a small nose). So I thought that maybe Pollack and friends had seen some other Middle Eastern actor and thought, *Hey, they all look the same, so just call the dude named Maz. He'll do.*

The first day I went to work on the film in New York I had a simple scene where I'm supposed to say a few lines to myself as I sit in my car, watching a suspect through binoculars. We did one take and Sydney Pollack's voice came over the walkie-talkie they put in the car with me.

"Do it again, but make it even more casual."

Take two and Pollack's voice: "This time, try a little more emphasis."

Take three: "You're trying too hard. Just throw it away."

Take four: "Breathe, relax, and say the lines."

At this point I'm melting, thinking, *They're going to fire me and I'll have to go back to playing terrorists. I knew they had the wrong guy! They wanted Ahmed! I can call him right now! Maybe I'll quit and become a chiropractor. I just hope no one's taken the license plate CHIRODK.*

By take seven we got it. And Pollack even came around and was joking with me by the end. The really cool thing with *The Interpreter* was that there was actually a scene where I'm on the bus, following the same suspect I was watching from my car before, and the bus explodes. I get off just before the explosion and survive. So it was one of the first times I had played a character who not only wasn't involved in the act of terrorism, but he actually survived it.

It was a bright day in the Jobrani family.

"You not die!" my mother said. "You didn't kill anyvon like I told you, but at least you not die. Remember, lights, camera, you go!"

Tehran, Iran

I first saw Tehran as a very, very young child, less than one second old, in fact. Which is a drawn-out way of saying: I was born there. I don't remember much because, like most babies, I was selfish and stupid and probably crying because one of my boundless needs was not being met exactly when I demanded it. I was born on Ashura, which is the day Shiite Muslims mourn the death of one of their prophets, Hussein. While I was crying in the hospital because I was being slapped on the ass, in the streets of Tehran people were crying because their prophet had been martyred years before. A day of crying—an inauspicious moment for the birth of a comedian.

My earliest memories as a kid in Tehran were of soccer, orange soda, Mohammad Ali, Zorro, Spider-Man, and chocolates. Yes, my experiences were very similar to those of a kid growing up in America. Even back then, America had done a tremendous job of exporting its culture abroad. We did not have the Iranian equivalent to Spider-Man or Superman or any other superhero, so I drank up Western culture wherever I found it. In Iran, that drink came in the color orange. Most people who find out I am originally from Iran think I grew up in a desert, riding camels and living near an oil well.

"Did you guys have camel traffic jams in the old country?"

"No," I'd say, "we didn't ride camels. And even if we did, there would be no camel traffic jams because there are no camel lanes. You just go around the guy on the slower camel."

"Well, you sure seem to know a lot about camels. There's no shame in admitting that you rode them as a kid back in Iran. Did you name your camels? In America, we sometimes name our cars."

"We didn't have camels!"

"Wow, someone's sensitive. Fine, you've never ridden a camel. Calm down."

"Okay, fine. I lied. I did ride a camel once. But that was at Marine World Africa USA! In Vallejo, California. USA! And his name was Bob."

The main difference between Iran and America, transportationally speaking, is that in the United States people actually follow traffic laws. When a car misses an exit, the motorist simply drives to the next exit, turns around and tries again. In Tehran when someone misses an exit, he puts the car in reverse right there on the freeway and goes backward. There is nothing scarier than being in the backseat of a car on a freeway and having the driver look at you as he drives in the wrong direction. All you hear are cars honking, drivers cussing, camels scurrying into the passing lane. You don't dare turn around to see what's speeding toward you, typically in the form of impending death moving at sixty-five miles an hour. Somehow, though, these eccentric drivers manage to zig-zag their way back to the missed exit and arrive safely at the proper destination. This has happened to me a few times in the Middle East, and I've learned that if you don't look back and just do some breathing exercises, you get through it fine. Just repeat this mantra: "I refuse to die going in reverse. I refuse to die going in reverse. I refuse to die . . ."

I don't know why people in the Middle East have no regard for traffic laws. However, I have a theory as to why New York City cabbies are notorious for being bad drivers. It's simple—the worst drivers from countries in the Middle East, Africa, and South America come to New York and get jobs as cab drivers. They are coming from places where going in reverse on the freeway is totally acceptable. When they arrive in New York, they implement this style of driving in city streets. New York cab driving is like the Indy 500 of bad drivers from around the world. The best of the best go there to compete. Or rather the worst of the worst, I sup-pose, depending on if you're the poor sap in the backseat.

My Dad, the Electricity Mogul

While I was enjoying my American-influenced youth, suddenly pro-tests began in the streets of my hometown in 1978. I didn't know what all the fuss was about. I was only six years old and too busy drinking orange soda to care. A year earlier, U.S. president Jimmy Carter had visited Tehran and made a famous speech where he called Iran an "island of stability in one of the more troubled areas of the world." One year later, Iran was in turmoil. It's safe to say Jimmy wasn't much of a fortune-teller. More of a misfortune teller.

Before I left for America, we would hear protests in the streets and have to observe a curfew every night. I remember being a kid and having to go into the basement a few times when the protests and gunfire got close to our house. I really didn't know what was happening. Mostly, I thought it was pretty cool to be with my family in the basement hiding from danger. I felt like Batman in the Batcave! (Yes, we had Batman in Iran, too. And no, he didn't ride a camel.)

My first six years in Iran were good ones. We lived on the same property as my grandmother, who would spoil my sister and me with gifts and sweets. My father made lots of money owning an electric company, so he had built a compound with two houses—one for us and one for my grandmother. Not an Osama bin Laden–like compound where we were hiding in plain sight by wearing white cowboy hats, but more of a benevolent compound. Do those exist? Why is it always bad guys who have compounds? We had a pool and a big grassy area where my cousins and I would play. I never really understood how my father came to own the electric company. I always thought I was the only one who never knew what his dad did until later in life I asked other people what their dads did. It's amazing how many people really don't know. I'm not sure if that's a reflection of the generation I grew up in or if it's an immigrant thing, but somehow dads didn't do a good job of giving their kids the full story.

"Dad, what do you do?"

"Make money."

"How?"

"Vork."

"What kind of work?"

"Vork that makes money. Eh-stop asking qvestions and eat deh food I paid for."

I was able to piece together stories to discover that my father had come from Tabriz, a city in the north of Iran, and moved to Tehran as a young man. He was employed at an electric company and slowly worked his way up until he was the boss. When the shah nationalized electricity in the 1950s and 1960s, his regime contracted out the work to a few companies, and one of those was my father's. I say 1950s or 1960s because my dad was never good at giving me the timeline of when anything happened.

"Hey Dad, when was I born?"

"Sometime in deh seventies."

"Early or late seventies?"

"Vhat am I, an accountant? You vere born. Be happy you're here."

My dad's company would get contracts to do the lighting for roads and buildings all over Iran. This helped him build considerable wealth and eventually become very powerful. When I describe my dad, I often reference Don Corleone from *The Godfather*. My dad was a rich, well-connected man; people would come to ask for favors and he would help them. As a kid I didn't know any of that. I only knew that whenever I needed money I would ask and he would hand me twenty- or hundred-dollar bills. This was where his indifference toward numbers worked in my favor.

"Hey Dad, can I get some cash?"

"How much do you need?"

"I don't know. Five, ten, a hundred."

"I'm no accountant. Take vhat you need. Give me back deh rest."

I was too young to ask why this man always had so much cash around. Was he a drug dealer? A stripper? An electric company CEO? He sure as hell was no accountant—he made that clear.

Escaping Revolution in First Class

I left Iran at age six for New York City, where my dad was on business. He was staying at the Plaza Hotel in a suite when my mother, my sister Mariam, and I joined him. We thought we would only be there for two weeks during our winter break, enough time to let the protests in Iran settle, but things never cooled down. We even left my baby brother, Kashi, back home and had to get him out later as things got worse. We packed for two weeks. We stayed for thirty years.

My first few months in America, my father would take business calls in the hotel room, forcing us to go shopping at FAO Schwarz or Macy's. One of my earliest purchases was an orange and white Snoopy winter set—a hat, scarf, and gloves. (I'm not joking. We Iranian children were OBSESSED with orange soda. The color orange became my favorite color. Anything I found with orange in it was something I loved.) I would spend the days running around Manhattan in my orange regalia and the nights going to dinners with my family ordering strawberries and whipped cream for dessert. I didn't know the details of the revolution taking place back in Iran, but it was working out fine for me. After all, I had escaped the revolution aboard a Pan Am flight, first class no less. In contrast, many of my friends had to escape through Pakistan or Afghanistan, spending years living a transient lifestyle while waiting for a visa to come to the West. Often when I hear these stories I feel guilty, so I try to compensate.

"It was so tough living across the street from FAO Schwarz when I first moved to America. Just to get to the toys I had to take the elevator down, wait for the light to turn green, and then cross traffic. And my dad typically gave me hundred-dollar bills so I was always having to make change. You know how hard that can be on an immigrant who barely knows how to do math in English?"

Iranians are like Lebanese or Cubans in that we are spread all around the world. Yes, there are millions of Iranians in Iran, but there is also a huge diaspora. When you come from a country that's had a revolution, or a monthly natural disaster, or simply a great deal of strife, it's good for your touring career because you are guaranteed to find people from your country wherever you go. If you're Iranian or Lebanese or Cuban, I advise you to pick up a guitar and learn to sing. Your audience is waiting for you.

I've done shows in Sweden, Norway, Australia, Dubai, Beirut, Canada, New York, Los Angeles, San Francisco, and even Kansas City. There's always at least one Iranian in every audience. How an Iranian ends up in Kansas City, I'll never know. Did he get off on the wrong flight? Was he kidnapped? What the hell is he doing in Kansas City? Nine times out of ten it has to do with college. Iranians are big on education, and since the 1950s, they would send their kids abroad to study. Some of the kids made it home to Iran. The unfortunate ones were stranded in Kansas City.

Happy New . . . WHAT? SPEAK UP!

Living in a diaspora has its pluses and minuses. One of the biggest minuses as a kid was that every Persian New Year we would have to call our relatives around the world and wish them a happy New Year. This seems like a simple enough task, but there's a catch. The Persian New Year is not like the Western New Year. In the West, it happens at midnight in each time zone around the world. So come midnight you scream, "Happy New Year!" to the people at your party, you kiss the person next to you, and then you post a message on Facebook and go to sleep. The Persian New Year is based on the Zoroastrian calendar and indicates the first moment of spring. So the moment occurs at the same time all around the world. Meaning it could occur at 3:26 p.m. in Iran, which would be 3:56 a.m. in California. I know this math seems a bit off, but Tehran is actually eleven and a half hours ahead of California. I don't know how they were able to split time zones into thirty-minute intervals, or why they would do such a thing. It's tough enough doing the math when you travel and have to convert money from dollars to Iranian rials. Whenever I travel anywhere outside the United States, I'm very confused for the entire first week. You give someone dollar bills and they give you what feels like Monopoly money. And the conversion is never basic math like 1:5 or 1:10. It's always 1:3.8675309. When dealing with Iran, you not only have to worry about converting the money, you also have to convert the time into thirty-minute intervals.

Back to the Persian New Year. Most normal people would let the family sleep and wake up the next morning to make their phone calls. Iranians are not normal. It is customary for younger family members to call older family members. So my dad would be up at 3:56 a.m. calling Iran and yelling into the phone. That's one thing I've never understood. Technology has made so much progress, but anytime you make a call to Iran, it feels like you're calling a village that just installed its first phone booth that week. To this day you must yell. Then there's a pause as your voice travels. Then you hear an echo of your voice. Then the person on the other end answers. After a few sentences you don't know if you're talking to yourself or to someone else. I assume part of the problem might be that someone from the government is listening to your call so maybe the third line is what's causing the difficulty in communication. I used to think that it was only Iran listening in on the calls, but I guess nowadays the United States might be listening, too. So that's four lines, which would further explain the bad quality and the need to shout.

Growing up, it was perfectly normal to wake up at four in the morning to your father shouting at relatives on the other side of the world. You would think he was mad at them, when in fact he was offering good wishes.

"I VISH YOU A GREAT NEW YEAR! VHAT? IIII VIIIIISH YOUUUUUUU A GREEEEAAAT NEW YEAAAAR! VHY ARE YOU REPEATING EVERYTING I'M SAYING? IS DAT ME TALKING OR YOU? I'M NOT YELLING! I SAID! I VISH YOU . . ."

This would go on for hours as we had to call relatives in Iran, Sweden, Kansas City—wherever the hell they were living. It was hard enough trying to sleep through this at four in the morning, but then my parents would wake us up to wish our relatives a happy New Year.

"HI! IT'S MAZ! MAZ! YOUR GRANDSON! WHY ARE YOU REPEATING EVERYTHING I SAY? IS IT MY TURN TO SHOUT OR YOURS?"

Living in the United States, phone calls were my main source of contact with Iran. I would get on the line with relatives and tell them how much I missed them. As I got older, it occurred to me I really didn't know them that well; it was just habit to say I missed them. Besides, it wouldn't have been too nice to tell the truth.

"HI. IT'S MAZ. I DON'T WANT TO BE ON THIS CALL. I BARELY KNOW YOU. IT'S BEEN YEARS SINCE I'VE SEEN YOUR FACE. I JUST REMEMBER YOU USED TO GIVE ME MONEY FOR CANDY. DON'T GET ME

WRONG, I APPRECIATED THAT, BUT I HONESTLY DON'T KNOW YOU THAT WELL AND MY DAD IS JUST MAKING ME TALK TO YOU AND TELL YOU I MISS YOU. WHY ARE YOU REPEATING EVERYTHING I SAY? I JUST WANT TO GO BACK TO BED. JUST HANG UP. HANG UP!"

Persian Eyes, They're Watching You

I did not return to Tehran until 1999. My father traveled there in the early 1990s to work on some real estate deals and earn back some money he had lost while living in the United States. In the ten years he was in America, he had lost much of his fortune in bad real estate ventures. It was strange seeing Don Corleone sitting around our condominium in Los Angeles, where we moved in 1990, waiting for the phone to ring, just staring at the wall very anxiously. I was always expecting him to pull me aside and whisper, "I should've known it was Barzini all along!"

Fortunately, he never went movie crazy. In Iran, if you lived rich, chances were that you would die rich. It was hard for someone on top to lose it all. In the United States, it was not the same. If you weren't careful with your money you could lose it very easily. And my father was not the type to put money into a 401(k) or a trust fund for the future. He was a self-made millionaire who thought he could never lose, but he had to move back to Tehran to get his business going again.

It wasn't until 1999 that my two brothers, sister, and I were able to get our papers in order to visit him. We had to arrange for visas that would allow us to come and go temporarily without having to serve in the military. Iran considers you a citizen of Iran even if you have become a citizen of another country, and they have mandatory military service for all boys of a certain age. So in order to visit we had to make sure our papers were cleared and we could enter the country without having to do military service.

I had no interest in becoming Jihad Joe. First of all, I am not into fighting for any military. The only one I could ever see myself joining would be Old Navy, and that's just because their sweatpants are comfy. Second, I grew up in America. Sure I spoke Farsi, but my reading and writing of the language was and is at the first grade level. I don't know what kind of a soldier I'd make if I couldn't even read the signs. "Mines to the left, water fountain to the right"—such a sign could result in very serious repercussions for me. I don't know how you spell "mines" nor "water fountain." I would hate to leave this world trying to drink water out of an improvised explosive device. Also, what would happen if one of the commanders wanted us to chant, "We hate America! Death to America!" Out of sincerity I would have to raise my hands and offer my opinion. "Sir, not all Americans are bad. You're right— some of them are real bastards. Still, I don't wish death upon anyone. Can we just say, 'Bad karma to all bad Americans'? That's more my style."

Visiting Iran made me realize that I wasn't as Iranian as I thought I was. In the United States, I didn't feel American enough, and in Iran I didn't feel Iranian enough. Somehow when strangers would see me in the streets they would know instantly that I had come from America.

"How's life in the United States?"

"How do you know I live there?"

"You're wearing Levi's five-o-one jeans. We don't have those here."

"You don't have jeans?"

"We have the five-o-twos. The five-o-ones are so 1998."

Being in Iran after twenty years was bittersweet. On the one hand, it was great to see Tehran and its beauty. It's a bustling city surrounded by the Alborz Mountains. It could really be a beautiful place were it not for the overpopulation and pollution. Obviously, under the current regime there's also a lack of basic freedoms. There's a lot of fear instilled in you, and you feel like you're being watched even when you're not. This made me very paranoid and forced me to walk around the streets with my hands up, constantly saying, "I didn't do it! Whatever you're thinking, I did not do it!" By the end of the second week I didn't trust anybody. My dad would come by my room at the end of the night.

"Goodnight, Son."

"Goodnight? What, exactly, do you mean by 'goodnight'?"

"Um . . . just goodnight?"

"Or maybe you mean I should go to sleep so you can look in my diary to see if I've written anything against the regime."

"Son, I don't vork for the regime."

"Sure you don't, Dad. Sure you don't."

When I went to visit it was the month of Ramadan, so we were supposed to fast during the daytime. None of my siblings or I are religious, so we weren't fasting. The only problem was that when we were out, we didn't want to be caught sneaking food. We would wait until we were in the car, and my dad would pass back cookies, which we would hide in our fists and eat surreptitiously, trying to look inconspicuous. I felt like an idiot, a grown man sneaking bites of lemon cookie with a vanilla cream center. They were delicious—delicious and blasphemous at the same time. I wonder what kind of deity cares if you have a cookie during holy daylight. Is there such a god? It's a shame how people can take a religious message and turn it into something so silly. I shouldn't have to feel guilty eating a cookie. Cookies are good whether you're Muslim, Jewish, or Christian. The only people who hate cookies are vegans! And even they have nondairy cookies.

Two weeks in Tehran during Ramadan was like being in junior high all over again. We were nervous eating our cookies during the day. We were nervous walking with our sister in the streets for fear that someone would stop us and ask about our relationship with her. In Iran, men are only supposed to be walking with a woman if they are engaged to her, or she is their mother, wife, or sister. The morality police could stop you and inquire as to your relationship to the girl you're walking with, and if they don't like your answer, they could throw you in jail. A lot of people who live in Tehran don't seem to fear this, but when you're visiting you're on high alert and freaked the hell out most of the time. I was constantly telling my sister to stay five steps behind. Then I realized this looked misogynistic, so I told her to stay five steps ahead. Which made it look like I was stalking her. We eventually settled on walking on opposite sides of the street, and I would occasionally shout chauvinistic barbs at her, just to fit in.

Of greater concern, alcohol is not allowed in Iran, although a lot of people drink it. The type that is consumed is either homemade or purchased from the Armenian black market. I did not dare drink in public, but the locals didn't seem to care. We went to dinner one night with an uncle who snuck in a flask. He told us all to order Cokes and then proceeded to spike our drinks. (They weren't actually Cokes, since Iran wouldn't import American products like Coca-Cola because of sanctions. It was a knockoff whose name I forget, but we'll call it Mullah-Cola.) Anyway, we were freaking out for fear we would get caught, but he was totally blasé. This was another stupid policy in Iran, where everyone knew people were breaking the law, but they did not want to admit it. If it weren't for the damn law I wouldn't even want a drink. But since my sixty-year-old uncle had gone to such lengths to sneak it in, I indulged.

Eight Minute Keb-Abs

The last time I was in Iran, my father took me to a gym. When I say gym, I mean sauna. And when I say sauna, I mean a place where men go to relax and pretend they are exercising. You can see the difference in cultures between the Middle East and the West when you go to exercise in these countries. In California, a gym is a place with treadmills and elliptical machines, free weights and dumbbells, men and women and mirrors everywhere. In Iran, a gym has one stationary bike, four dumbbells, an enormous sauna and steam room, and men only—no women allowed. There are gyms for women, too, but I would have had to dress in drag to get into those.

It was amazing how little thought was given to the actual exercise room at the gym and what detail had gone into the sauna area. There was a sauna, a steam room, a cold bath, a hot bath, and even a restaurant to eat rice and kebab after you've steamed. "Exercisers" go in, sweat out the pounds, then come out and put them right back on. Thankfully, I was there during Ramadan, so the restaurant was closed. Besides, I had eaten so many contraband cookies, I wouldn't have been able to stomach a post-workout kebab.

Men go to these places to spend the day together and get away from their families. They talk politics, sports, and finance and leave feeling like they've gotten an actual workout when in reality the only reason they sweat is because it's so hot. I was shocked at how openly these guys were talking politics and criticizing the leadership. People had gotten to a point where they didn't give a crap. And they knew so much detail about everyone in the regime. I think it's a cultural thing, but Iranians will know every nuance about a person and his background. Whereas in America you work with a guy for ten years and never know his last name.

"Hey Mike! How's the wife and kids? You don't have a wife and kids? Your name is Ted? Are you sure?"

In Iran people know first names, last names, family history, what car you drive, net worth, where you went to school, why you went to school, whom you slept with at school, who wouldn't sleep with you at school, on and on. I don't know why Iranians know so many details about each other, but I'm guessing it's in case they want to set you up to marry their daughter. It's like buying a new car. They do all the research so they can compare and contrast. Why set your daughter up with a Toyota when she could be with a BMW?

That trip to see my dad was the last time I visited Iran, which is a shame. I've done stand-up all over the Middle East, but I have never done it in my birth country. It is a dream of mine to one day be able to perform there. For now, though, I don't know if the current regime would welcome me because I've made fun of them in my stand-up. I'm guessing they would have me begin my show with a confession that I am a puppet for the Great Satan and close by denouncing Jerry Seinfeld. "He is a Jew. And the only thing worse than a Jew is a gay. While we're at it, Ellen DeGeneres, go to hell!"

As an Iranian-American stand-up comedian, it is almost impossible not to talk about Iran in your act. That's because Iran is always in the news in the United States. Even when something happens that has nothing to do with Iran, Iran will find a way to work itself into the discussion. There was a revolution in Egypt in 2011, and the first thing Iran did was send ships into the Suez Canal. They weren't dropping anything off or picking anything up. They just made the trip to indicate that under the new Egyptian leadership, they would be treated as closer allies. Either way, the revolution was about Egypt, but Iran got its name into the papers. The Iranian regime must have the same publicist as the Kardashians.

Being unable to avoid talking about Iran makes it difficult to go back and visit. I do one joke in which I claim that perhaps the leadership in Iran is on drugs. That would explain why they talk so much shit to America—a country with the most powerful military in the world. The fact is that opium usage is high in Iran, so it would make sense that some of these leaders *could* actually be on drugs. We always assume that leaders of a country have their act together. But anyone who witnessed Muammar Gaddafi's last days in power in Libya understands that a lot of these guys are out of their minds. Gaddafi was rambling on like a meth head. I'm convinced that some leaders in Iran are just as bad. And the fact that I just wrote that line means I won't be performing stand-up in Iran anytime soon. I'm not sure if I'm officially banned in Iran, but if I ever do a show out there I plan to call it *"Banned in Iran?"* and just perform until they arrest me. At that point the tour will change its name to *"Banned in Iran!"* Exclamation, end of paragraph, end of tour.

The Supreme Newsletter

In 2009, there were protests in the streets of Tehran after the presidential elections. Many accused the regime of rigging the elections and giving President Ahmadinejad a wide victory when it was expected to be a close race. In some provinces, Ahmadinejad got more than 100 percent of the votes. Apparently some people voted in more than one province. The whole thing reeked of voter fraud. The protests became known as the Green Movement. Iranians were proud to see the peaceful protests, and for once it was okay to say you were Iranian in America. Up until then, most Iranians preferred to say they were Persian because it sounded nicer and friendlier. It distanced you from the current regime, and also most Americans didn't even know what you were talking about. "You're Parisian? I love french fries!"

I remember being in Chicago for the Just for Laughs comedy festival and a big announcement came from the Supreme Leader of Iran claiming that if people continued to protest, whatever happened to them would be out of his hands. It was basically a threat that the authorities would be allowed to punish the protesters any way they saw fit. That really pissed me off. How dare he make such a declaration against his own people? And what the hell is a Supreme Leader anyway? What is this, *Star Wars*? I'm willing to accept a supreme burrito, but a Supreme Leader? Give me a break!

After the announcement, the protests went south as the regime cracked down and turned to violence to stop the movement. People were shot and many died in pursuit of democracy. I observed the news daily, like a soap opera I couldn't take my eyes off—a violent, bloody, real-life *Dallas*. I would go to bed late at night after reading as much as I could about the movement online, and wake up the next morning to CNN to see if any progress had been made. One clip that kept playing on the news was of a young woman, Neda Agha-Soltan, dying after being shot by the authorities. It was a poignant and sad scene to watch. I decided I would go to Iran and join the protesters in the streets to fight for our freedoms. No, I didn't really do that. I'm a comedian. Not a lunatic. And I have no experience overthrowing regimes. What I do have, however, is a monthly newsletter, which had until then been intended to inform people about my upcoming shows.

The newsletter went out to thousands of people and usually elicited only a few responses. This time, I dedicated the whole thing to my support of the Green Movement and asked others to please support it any way they could. I hit send and went to sleep, having done my part to support Democracy in the Middle East. The next morning I awoke to hundreds of responses. Most expressed their support. However, I also got some people challenging me. One e-mail came from a woman in Greece. How she got on my e-mail list I have no idea. She basically told me that if the people of Iran had voted for Mahmoud Ahmadinejad, then who was I to question it. She said that this was all a ploy by the West to overthrow the regime and that I should mind my own business.

This upset me—not just because she claimed it was none of my business, but that someone had the gall to question the Supreme Word of my newsletter. This led to an e-mail exchange that consumed hours of my life—hours that I could have used to write jokes about Ahmadinejad! After several exchanges I thought, *What the hell am I doing? I'm debating some chick in Greece who has no influence over any of this. Why do I care what she thinks?* It took a lot for me to stop myself from responding to her last e-mail. What can I say—I'm a man, I need to get in the last word. I finally let it go,

Tiburon, California

I'm Iranian, but I grew up white. That's because I was raised in Tiburon, California, across the bay from San Francisco. Tiburon is a very affluent and gentrified city in Marin County, where the mountain bike was invented—at least that's what Wikipedia has to say on the matter. Mountain biking is a very white sport. When most Iranians hear "mountain" they think hiking or horseback riding—usually as a means of escaping Iran. When Iranians hear "biking" they think of riding on a flat surface. I'm guessing whoever decided to mix mountains with biking was an open-minded, adventure-seeking, and most likely stoned white dude. "Bro, you know that mountain we can barely walk up without falling off the cliff? Why don't we try to ride a bike up it?"

Growing up, most of my friends were white with a few Persians sprinkled in here and there. Before I go any further, I know that any Iranians reading this right now are thinking: *But Iranians ARE white!* That is true. Iranians are ethnically white. The word "Iran" derives from the word "Aryan." Our ancestors can be traced back to the Caucasus, so that makes us Caucasian—the original white people. Yes, Aryans were originally dark complexioned people with thick, hairy eyebrows. This is a point that many educated Iranians in the West insist on making. It's for this reason that when the census comes out every ten years, Iranians continue to mark the box that reads "white" and move on with their lives. Based on the last census in 2010, there are about 300,000 Iranians in America. Based on my personal experiences in Westwood, California, there are at least 300,000 Iranians at most Persian weddings. There have been estimates of between 300,000 and 1.5 million Iranians in America. The reason for this wide discrepancy is that Iranians are not into filling out census forms. That's because they want to lay low and avoid the government.

"If you tell deh government you're here, den vhen deh next revolution comes dey vill know vhere to find you."

Many Iranians throw away census forms when they appear at their homes. If they do fill out the form, they try to be as vague as possible:

Age: 0
How many people live in your household? 0 or so
Income: About 0
Ethnic background? Vhite. Or Italian. Or whichever ethnicity is not
    currently making headlines.

In the West, despite our Caucasian heritage, Iranians are seen as more brown than white. If you don't believe me, try this test.

Get an Iranian with a thick Persian accent and a unibrow and have him run up to the front of an airplane before the doors close for takeoff and tell the stewardess he doesn't feel well and needs to get off the plane. No matter what, he has to *insist* that he needs to get off and he needs to make a big scene until they let him off. If the police don't show up to arrest this man then I will give you your money back for this book.

Recently, I was on a plane and a white American girl did this exact thing. No fuss was made. The crew let her off the plane, thanked her for almost flying that airline, and we took off. The passenger next to me asked, "Shouldn't they stop the plane and remove any baggage that girl might have checked in? What if she had a bomb in her suitcase?" I smiled and replied, "Nah, she's white. No bombs, but probably lots of mood stabilizers. We'll be okay." So brown equals terrorist and white equals one individual crackpot who just really wants to get off the plane.

Growing up in Tiburon, there were so few Persians that if you ran into one it was an occasion for celebration. One time in high school I cut class with a baseball teammate who had the whitest name ever—good old American Mark—and we went to get a sandwich before the game. We ended up at a deli where the owners turned out to be Iranian. I could tell from the Persian accent that the old man behind the counter was a fellow countryman, but I decided to play it cool. I was trying to blend in and I didn't want to remind Mark, or myself, that I was Iranian. The old man looked at my dark complexion and tilted his head.

"Vhere are you ferom, young man?" he asked in a thick accent.

Trying to sound as American as possible, I responded, "Tiburon, dude."

"Yes, but vhere are you *ferom* ferom?" This meant, "Don't try to bullshit me, son. I know you're a foreigner, just like me."

Still, I tried to be coy. "Oh, *from* from? Downtown Tiburon."

"Yes, but vhere are you *ferom ferom* ferom?"

The guy was relentless.

"*From from* from? You mean originally? Like where was I born?"

Even White Mark leaned in for my reply. He knew the answer but was confused about why I was acting so evasive.

"Fine, I'm from Iran. There, I said it! You happy, old man?"

Not only was he happy, he was ecstatic. It was as if he'd found a long-lost son. "Iran! I knew it! Me too! Dees eez gereat. Here, have a free cookie!"

"Free cookie?"

"Two free cookies. Von for your vhite ferend!"

This was always happening whenever we walked into an Iranian-owned business. Once we got cookies, once we got ice cream, often we'd get hugs. Mark enjoyed the benefits: "Dude, I love hanging out with you. We're always getting free shit!" "Yes," warned the skeptical Iranian side of me, "but don't get comfortable. Today they're offering cookies, tomorrow it'll be their daughters. They're setting us up for something."

My Parents, the Foreigners

Growing up with an Iranian family in a predominantly white county can present its own set of problems. No matter how hard I tried to blend in, my parents always managed to show up and give away the fact that I was different. When my friends were picked up from soccer practice, usually one parent would arrive to retrieve them. Often, my friends had parents who were divorced, which was totally cool in America. However, with Iranians, that was a no-no. No matter how much your parents hated each other, or could not stand each other even for short durations, they had to hang in there and save face in the community.

"My vife? Do I love her? Love is such a relative term. I tell you now dat ve live in de same house together and at least vonce a veek ve say hello to von another."

Even if my Iranian parents had fallen out of love, they would both come to pick me up from soccer and they would bring the entire family with them in one car—mom, dad, siblings, aunts, grandma, neighbors, roosters. If you ever see a car overloaded with people, breaking all kinds of occupancy and seat-belt laws with several generations of a family crammed in wherever there's room, they're either Mexicans or Iranians. We bring the whole village for every single errand. I'm not sure why that is, but perhaps it has something to do with the revolutions and bad political circumstances our people fled in the old country. We pack the car with the entire family in case a revolution breaks out between the time we leave the house and the time we get to the soccer field. That way, if the revolution does happen (which in our minds is inevitable), we'll have the whole family in the car and can keep on driving until we get to the next country.

Even if my parents ever came alone to pick me up from soccer, they still stood out. My father had ways of being noticed. As an example, he drove a Rolls-Royce Silver Shadow. "Rolls-Royce?" you might say. "How lucky." No. There was nothing lucky about being the rich kid from Iran whose dad drove a Rolls-Royce during the Iran hostage crisis in America.

For those of you who are too young to remember and too lazy to google this historic event, here are the CliffsNotes. Iran had a revolution in 1979. Many Iranians, including my family and me, fled the country and came to America to get away from the Islamic regime that took over. No sooner had we settled in than a group of Iranian students stormed the American embassy in Iran and took fifty-two American hostages for 444 days, which was when . . . oh hell, just rent *Argo*, starring Ben Affleck as the lead CIA agent who happens to come from a Mexican background and rescues a bunch of good-guy Americans from a bunch of evil Iranians, which leads to him landing the role of Batman in the *Batman vs. Superman* movie. (Iranians like taking credit for everything, so, yes, I'm taking credit for helping Ben land Batman.) In the late seventies, there weren't a thousand channels on TV. So every night Americans tuned in to watch Ted Koppel and his red coif tell us: "Day one hundred . . ." "Day one hundred and fifty-two . . ." "Day three hundred . . ." All I could think was: *How long is this damn thing going to last? And how does Ted Koppel get his hair to sit like a perfectly manicured squirrel?*

Marin County was filled with rich white people who tended to be low key with their fortunes. They would drive Volvos and Saabs; some would even ride bikes. Yes, mountain bikes! My father, on the other hand, decided to buy the Rolls and drive around town like a rich Saudi sheikh. It wasn't bad enough that there was a hostage crisis being played out every day on TV and that all my classmates likely thought I was the most spoiled kid in the school. But then my dad had to drop me off and pick me up in this gaudy car he had bought from a friend. My dad purchased most of his possessions from friends. Anyone who had financial problems would come to our house with items to sell and he would buy them. He was like eBay before there was eBay. He came home with old cars, ill-fitting suits, and anything else that was on the market. One time he brought home a bunch of phones. We already had plenty of phones, and we certainly didn't have a bunch of extra rooms for the new phones. So they just sat in a cupboard in the kitchen waiting to go extinct. My mom made sure to remind him of his wasteful ways anytime they got into an argument.

"Have you thought about buying some new used phones for us? Zee ones in zee cupboard are getting dusty. And vhile you're at it, vhy don't you get some more undersized suits so ve can give dem avay de next time some fancy midgets visit us?"

I-ran, I-ran So Far Away

During the Iran hostage crisis, my number-one goal was to lay low, blend in, and find more friends with names like Mark, Bret, Jesse, Steve, and Chip. I didn't want anyone to know I was different, and I sure as hell didn't want the older kids to know that I was Iranian, which even back then equated to "terrorist." That would just give them an extra body to beat up. I didn't even want anyone to know I existed. The less they knew about me, the better my chances of making it through the school days and getting home without a broken nose. Pops and his Rolls didn't help in this mission at all.

My attempt at blending in failed miserably when I was in the fourth grade. I was met with a verbal confrontation by a sixth grader named Jim who somehow figured out that I was the representative of the Islamic Republic of Iran in Marin County. After all, I had a funny name, beautiful furry eyebrows, strange-sounding parents, and a dad who drove a better car than his dad. I had to be involved with the hostage crisis somehow—I looked the part. This sixth grader came up with a clever nickname, calling me a Fucking Eye-ranian. That's what people called Iranians back then: Fucking

Eye-ranians. "First of all," I explained, "it's pronounced Ee-ron-ian, not Eye-ranian. Second, you're bigger than me so it's whatever you want it to be. Third, I'm not sure where you heard a rumor that I'm Iranian. I'm not. I'm totally Italian—*ciao!*"

Such were the times that my only recourse was to stand there and take Jim's abuse. The only person who came to my defense was a slightly older black fifth grader. I don't remember his name, but I remember him walking with me and telling me to turn the other cheek and not take it personally. Given his advice, let's call him Martin Luther King Junior Junior. MLKJJ had gone through similar abuse and learned to deal with it. In his case, he was a big kid, so I'm guessing that's why the abuse toward him eventually ceased. I made a mental note to start lifting weights as soon as possible. Who knew how long this hostage thing would last? I either had to grow biceps or learn more words in Italian. You could only fool so many people with "*ciao!*" "spaghetti!" "tortellini carbonara!" It was a race between my biceps growing and Jim coming up with a clever new insult the other kids would latch onto.

Then disaster struck, in the form of A Flock of Seagulls, the eighties band that wrote a song that gave kids plenty of ammunition in their bigotry arsenal: "I Ran (So Far Away)." For any non-Iranians reading this book, it was unfortunate to go right from the hostage crisis to this song. The lyrics had nothing to do with Iran, but kids would drag out the two words to make fun of me by singing, "I-ran, I-ran so far away." It was like fingernails on a chalkboard.

"It's Ee-ron, goddamn it! Ee-ron. Get your racial barbs right."

"Oh, look who's the angry Eye-ranian now!"

Years later, while doing stand-up comedy, I began talking about these incidents. It felt like I was opening up an old wound, but it was good to talk about the childhood troubles I had with Jim. I was telling the Fucking Eye-ranian tale around the world on my Brown and Friendly tour. I would end the story by telling the audience that the kid who teased me back then had no idea I would become a stand-up comedian, performing in front of thousands of people some nights, and that I would tell them, "Ladies and gentlemen, Jim Juvonen is an asshole. Please spread the word on Facebook and Twitter and wherever else you like." I began outing this kid, now presumably an adult, and the audience loved it because everyone can identify with being bullied at some point in his or her life.

Still, part of me felt bad because I figured this was an incident that happened when we were kids. That's what kids do, pick on each other. Who knows, maybe if there had been a North Korean in our school I would've picked on him, or at least diverted attention to him so that Jim and company would leave me alone. "Hey, Jim, I know I'm a fuckin' eye-Ranian, but did you hear what the North Korean kid said about you? Yeah, plus he's a communist! Get him!" I knew Jim was older now and probably a family man who was just living his life. The last thing he needed was to be hassled by me and my fans. I wondered what he was up to. Then one day, when I was listening to an interview on NPR with another Jim, comedian Jimmy Fallon, my question was answered. The interviewer asked Fallon about his short-lived movie career. He responded that he was in a few flops, but the one good thing that did come out of his movie career was *Fever Pitch*, where he met Drew Barrymore's producing partner and married her. The name of the woman he married was Nancy Juvonen. My jaw dropped. It's an unusual name. Could Fallon have married someone related to Jim Juvonen, who made my year as a fourth grader a living hell? I did what any self-respecting American would do. I googled it. Turns

one time we went to an ice cream parlor. My mouth was watering for my favorite flavor—strawberry with chocolate sprinkles. The girl behind the counter turned out to be a few years older than me and suddenly, everything changed. My father broke into a deep laugh and—very loudly, extremely embarrassingly—began hitting on the girl on my behalf.

"HELLO, YOUNG LADY. YOU ARE LOOKING FOR HUSBAND, YES? MY SON VIL BE YOUR HUSBAND. HA! HA! HA!"

He sounded like the bald black guy from the 7UP commercials in the eighties. (If you don't know who I'm talking about, just search online for "Bald black guy from 7UP." He was a classic!) When your father walks into an ice cream parlor and starts arranging your marriage—at the age of ten, mind you—you turn the color of the strawberry ice cream you were planning to order.

"YOU MARRY MY SON, I DRIVE YOU IN MY ROLLS-ROYCE TO HONEYMOON!"

My mother was subtler in her ways, which, given that my dad was so loud and grand, wasn't saying much. The image most Americans have of Iranian women is of gentle, docile, veiled ladies who cook, clean, and raise the kids. My mother was far from that. She was a beautiful, active, and tough lady who did not hesitate to take her hangers and beat the crap out of me, my sister, my brothers, and even my aunt who lived with us. She wasn't as bad as Joan Crawford from *Mommie Dearest*, but when we messed around she let us have it. This was a reflection of our culture. I thought this was normal in every family until one day when I was at my American friend Jesse's house. His mom yelled at him for something, and Jesse, to my dismay, yelled back. I held my breath, waiting for his mom to whip out her hangers and beat the crap out of her son, and perhaps me. Instead she just yelled back at Jesse and went about her business.

I was shocked. "That's it? That's all she's going to do?"

"Yep."

"No beatings with a hanger?"

"Why would she beat me with a hanger?"

"Because she's your mom. That's what moms do, isn't it?"

I'm not sure if this was only an Iranian thing or if it's an immigrant thing, but beatings were a natural part of my upbringing. My father never hit us. He would just raise his voice and, due to the baritone delivery, we would immediately pee in our pants. My mother, on the other hand, had a repertoire of hanger abuse, spankings, and ear pulling. I'm convinced that my ears were naturally much smaller but that she helped shape them to the Spock-like size they are today.

In the modern world that we live in, hitting your kids is a big no-no. I would never hit my kids, but sometimes I can understand why our parents would hit us. You get much quicker results when you come out of your room wielding a hanger in your hand than in the current environment, when you pull your child aside, get down to his level, and try to speak to him with a calm voice: "Do you know why Daddy is upset? Was it a good idea to pee pee on Daddy's computer? Please go to your room and think about what you did. You don't want to go to your room? Okay, let's talk about how going to your room makes you feel."

As a kid I felt like I was living with a bunch of foreigners. Looking back on it, I was. When you come to a country at the age of six, you adapt quickly to the culture. However, your parents aren't as exposed to the natives as you are. Older immigrants tend to find other immigrants to hang out with. We were always going to the homes of the other three or four Iranian families in Marin. They also had kids my age, so we could get together and play while our parents indulged in Persian card games. This gave us ample time to bad-mouth them and exchange strategies on how to distance ourselves further.

"The worst part of having an Iranian dad is that he wears too much cologne," someone would complain. "Whenever he picks me up from soccer, I can smell him a mile away."

"You think you have it bad? My dad insists on playing backgammon in the park while he waits for me to finish my practice."

"You want fresh off the boat? My dad drives me around town in a Rolls-Royce and proposes marriage to thirteen-year-old girls on my behalf. He thinks he's the shah."

Call Me Tony

Kids often turn to film and TV to find people they can relate to. Nowadays, when my kids watch TV there are cartoons with Latino leads (*Dora the Explorer*), Asian leads (*Ni Hao Kai-Lan*) and bear leads (*Little Bear*). Being Iranian in America in the eighties, I didn't find many people on TV who I could relate to. There was the Iron Sheik, who was a wrestling villain from the World Wrestling Federation. He was hard to cheer for because he would come on TV with his Russian counterpart, Nikolai Volkoff, and shout, "Iran number von! Russia number von! America?" Then he would spit on the canvas. The crowd would boo and Hulk Hogan would arrive and distribute ass-whoopings for all the little Hulkamaniacs out there. The only other Iranians on TV or in film were the rich Persian neighbors in *Down and Out in Beverly Hills* and the Iranian husband in *Not Without My Daughter*.

For anyone who hasn't seen *Not Without My Daughter*, let me summarize. It is based on a true story and stars Sally Field, who is married to an Iranian man in America. The Iranian man is played by Alfred Molina, who looks more Persian than I do. (I actually took a Shakespearean acting class with him once and he was so nice that any animosity I felt toward him from being in this movie melted away.)

While they're in the United States, the Molina character, Sayed Bozorg Mahmoody, a.k.a. Moody, is a charming medical school student who seems lovely to Sally. He has romantic picnics with her and treats her like his queen. Then they go for a short trip to Iran and the guy changes on a dime. He becomes misogynistic and abusive. (Which I guess explains why they call him "Moody.") He won't let Sally out of the house and tells her that he's going to kill her and sacrifice her like a sheep. Furthermore, Moody tells her, he won't let her take their daughter back to the United States. So Sally sets out to find a way to escape with her child, and thus the title, *Not Without My Daughter*.

This was in Sally Field's heyday; it would be like a Middle Eastern man doing this to Reese Witherspoon today. This movie did more to hurt the dating lives of Iranian men in America than the hostage crisis. Many of my friends relinquished any pride they had in their Persian background and just pretended to be Italian. Somehow, they could handle the hostage crisis, they could manage "I Ran (So Far Away)," but *Not Without My Daughter* put them over the edge. They went from being named Shahrokh, Mahmoud, and Farsheed to all being named Tony. I'm not sure why they all chose Tony, but it seemed odd to me that women wouldn't question you when you would introduce your friends this way: "I'm Maz. This is my friend Tony. Over there, next to Tony, is Tony. Over there next to Tony and Tony is Tony. Yes, they're all Italian. Very Italian. Me? I'm Iranian. Wait, where are you going? Did I say Iranian? I meant Persian, like the cat. Meow!"

Finding Italian heroes on TV was easy. I became a fan of every Italian actor. If their names ended with an "o" I was into them—Robert De Niro, Al Pacino, Marlon Brando, Elmo. (Okay, Elmo wasn't around back then, but if he had been, I would've worshipped him!) This love of everything Italian became an obsession for my friends and me. It was so easy, and acceptable, to be Italian. First of all, Italians have a lot in common with Iranians. We both are dark-haired macho types who like to wear gold chains and show off our hairy chests. We both put a lot of emphasis on family and food. And we both live with our parents until we're married. Add the fact that most Americans did not speak Italian and we were set. All we had to do was speak Persian with an Italian accent and women would be so impressed they would practically throw themselves at us. We just added an "a" or an "o" to the end of every word and threw in words like *ciao* and *bella*. We were careful not to use too many Persian words with the guttural "khhhh" sound in them. That would raise suspicion.

"Okay, *bella*, let's stopp-o the talk-o and maka da love. Khhhhh-okay? I mean . . . okay-o?"

All This Time I Was White

When people meet me, they often assume I am fully immersed in the Persian culture and I am more Iranian than American. But when I reflect on my life, I realize I have spent most of it in America—and most of it surrounded by American friends. Their influence on me can be seen in many ways. For example, I have a

401(k). Most Iranians from the old country don't even know what that is. When I talk to my mother about my 401(k), she thinks I'm talking about the new Mercedes.

Another American pastime that I took up as a child was baseball. I don't know if I played this sport because I loved it or if I was trying to fit in. I didn't realize how foreign baseball was to Iranians until I tried to explain the game to my grandfather. He would see me leaving the house with my mitt and bat: "Vhere are you going vith dat shovel?" For some reason he called the bat a shovel. It looks nothing like a shovel, but I guess he figured I was off to dig with it. To him the mitt must've been a gardening glove. I would explain that the bat is used to hit a ball and then you have to run around a diamond and make it back home. This just confused him more. "Vhy do you run around before you come home? Just come home. And if you see diamond, don't run. Pick up. I have friend. He get us good money."

The American-ness of baseball, and eventually my 401(k), were trumped by the American-ness of my choice to become an actor. This, to my Iranian parents, was the most foreign thing they had ever heard. "You vant to be actor? Vhat the hell does dat mean? Are you gay?" Persian parents, for the most part, don't believe in their children pursuing dreams. To a Persian parent, there are only a few options in life, and those include lawyer, doctor, engineer, or, preferably, an engineering lawyer with a medical degree. Anything else, the community will frown upon. From an early age my dad would encourage me to be a lawyer. "You go to law eh-school. You get your degree. You vork for me." Just like *The Godfather*. He wasn't so much interested in a son as he was a consigliere.

The idea of becoming an actor came to me when I was twelve. At the time, Eddie Murphy was huge, and I wanted to be just like him. I participated in my school's musical in the seventh grade and sang and danced my way to the lead the following year, where I got to play Li'l Abner. Whenever I was onstage, I felt alive. It was as fun for me to do plays as it was to play soccer and baseball, which were my other loves. My parents tried to be supportive, but I always felt that they were uncomfortable seeing me act.

They would come to my plays in obnoxious outfits. This being Marin County, most of the other parents showed up dressed nicely, but casual. My parents, on the other hand, had to stand out. It was as if they were out for a night at the Met. My dad would be in a suit and tie, my mom in a beautiful dress, my aunt in a mink coat, the rooster in a new vest—everyone was excited to be out for a night on the town. They would sit in the audience and watch, probably understanding every third word that came out of my mouth. I don't think my parents ever really *got* what the plays were about, but they sat politely and clapped when they heard the cue.

My aunt, who was younger and understood the plays, couldn't control her excitement. Every little thing that I did would warrant a standing ovation from her with a loud, "BRAVO Maziyar! Bravo!" Later in life I would learn to appreciate people yelling "bravo" from the audience, but at the age of twelve, living with a family of immigrants you were trying to distance yourself from, it was mortifying. I would be onstage and see my aunt standing in the audience. She looked like a lighthouse in the middle of the ocean. Everyone could see her. And they sure as hell could hear her. I would be trying to deliver my lines but also wanting to interrupt the play to deal with the disturbance. Namely, my family. My original hecklers.

"ENOUGH! All I did was recite a line. You can't clap every time I say something! You're making the show go long! Someone please grab this lady by her mink coat and escort her to the exit. Security?"

It took fourteen years to convince my parents that being an actor and comedian was an honorable profession. I was twenty-six when they finally accepted there was nothing they could do about it. "Deez damn Americans and their liberal vays," they told each other, "have finally turned our son gay!" Choosing acting as my life's profession was very much like what I imagine it would be to come out of the closet. At first they were both in denial. My father, who was living in Iran by that time, would continue to remind me on the phone that I should be going back to graduate school to get my Ph.D. in political science. "Vhen you go back and get your Ph.D. den you can go to law eh-school and den you can come vork for me."

"Dad, I'm not going back."

"Look, if you're gay, just say you're gay."

"I'm not gay."

"Den dat settles it. You vill get your degree and vork for me."

"So if I were gay I couldn't work for you?"

"So you ARE gay? I knew it!"

My mother would wait for opportunities to recommend other jobs I could pursue that had a secure future. She had given up on professions that the community would not look down upon and just wanted me to consider jobs that I could at least do in other countries. "How about learning to fix vashing machines? Vashing machines are alvays bereaking down. And if dere's ever a revolution in the U.S., you can alvays fix vashing machines in Argentina."

It wasn't until we moved to Los Angeles in the early nineties that becoming a professional actor started to feel like a real option. It was also where I started to embrace my Persian culture. Los

Angeles has the highest concentration of Iranians outside of Iran. Whereas in Marin running into an Iranian was a big deal, in L.A. it was common. When I first moved down I got a job in a Warehouse record store. (For any teenagers who happen to be reading this, there used to be actual stores where we bought our music. And back then we actually talked to a salesperson, who would give us a plastic bag without charging us ten cents for it. Those were wild times.) One day at the store I ran into an Iranian who was about the same age as me. I had learned from Marin that saying hello to a fellow Iranian could get you free things, or at least some hugs.

"Are you Iranian?" I asked.

"Yes."

"So am I!" I held out my arms for an embrace.

"So?"

"Don't you want to hug?"

"What are you, a freak?"

"No. I just figured since we're both Iranians we should hug."

"Look around you. The whole place is Iranian."

"Wait. What's your name?

"Tony."

"An Iranian named Tony!"

"And that's my friend Tony. And over there, that's my other friend, Tony."

It was as if I had finally come home.

Los Angeles, California

Moving to Los Angeles from Northern California was a culture shock to me, much as I imagine it would be for someone from the Midwest. Growing up in Northern California, it was ingrained in us to hate Los Angeles. We were the cool, down-to-earth, lovey-dovey Californians, and Angelenos were the superficial, over-tanned, annoying Californians. They were the hip place everyone in the world had heard of; we were the suburbs. They drove red Ferraris; we drove green Saabs (except for my dad, who, of course, drove the Rolls-Royce, throwing off this entire theory).

My family had moved into a high-rise on Wilshire Boulevard in Westwood, the Iranian Jeffersons. All of the high-rises on that boulevard were packed with Iranians. One family must have moved into a condo sometime in the 1950s, then word got out and one by one everyone came—cousins, neighbors, aunts, grandparents, roosters. It's amazing how long a cousin can live out of a suitcase. They come for a week and stay for decades. Whenever you step out of an elevator in a Westwood high-rise your nose is instantly infused with smells of kebabs, saffron, and *shambalileh*, which are fenugreek leaves. They are an ingredient in a dish called *ghormeh sabzi*, which is a green broth that we put over white rice and one of the most delicious foods known to mankind. It's the Iranian equivalent of gravy.

Persian food is generally some of the best food in the world. If you've never had it, find your nearest restaurant, order *ghormeh sabzi*, chicken kebabs, and the burnt rice at the bottom of the pan called *tah deeg*. (I know it sounds horrible, but it's delicious.) And always—ALWAYS—check the bill at the end of the meal because they may try to inflate it. A rule of thumb: If the Persian waiter keeps calling you "my friend" during the meal, chances are you're going to get overcharged. This is true when dealing with Middle Easterners in any transactional situation. As soon as they call you "my friend," put your wallet away, back out slowly, then run to the most American establishment you can find—a Sbarro, or an all-you-can-eat Chinese food buffet. Remember, they are NOT your friend.

I had this happen to me when I visited Morocco years ago. Having grown up in Marin County, I had forgotten the "my friend" rule when a rug salesman invited me into his store to have an innocent look at his wares.

"My friend, come look at my rugs."

"Wow, that's so nice. Sure, I'll come in."

After a few minutes, I was checking out the rugs and thinking what a pleasant afternoon it had turned into.

"My friend, which ten rugs would you like to buy today?"

"Ten rugs? I'm sorry, my friend, but I live in a small room in my mother's condo. The room already has a carpet, so I don't really have anywhere to put any rugs."

"No problem, my friend. Tell me—which three rugs you would like to buy?"

"You don't understand, my friend. I don't have any space. Not even for one rug."

"My friend, you buy today for twelve hundred dollars. You sell tomorrow at a great profit in the United States. Just buy, my friend."

He had doubled up on his "my friends," which made the whole thing more confusing. How can you resist two "my friends" in one paragraph? I ended up buying three rugs. I had nowhere to put them, but I had convinced myself this stranger was giving me good financial advice because he had repeatedly called me his friend. What do you do with three Moroccan rugs when you're living in a small bedroom in the corner of your mother's condo? You try to sell them to your friends and family—that's what you do! For the next six months, I drove around Los Angeles with a stack of Moroccan rugs in the trunk of my car. Anytime I was at a party, a picnic—any social gathering, really—and there was the slightest opening, I started pushing those rugs.

"My friend," I would begin, "you look like you need a good rug. Come look in the trunk of my car. Which two would you like to buy today, my friend?"

Unfortunately, being from the old country, most of my relatives never fell for this trick.

"I am not your ferend. I am your modder. And you live in *my* house, so eh-stop terying to sell me your eh-stupid rugs."

In the end I just gave the rugs away as gifts and made a

whopping zero dollars on my investment. I would've done better if I'd invested in Lehman Brothers. "My friend, which three subprime loans would you like to buy?"

Grandpa's Dirty Mouth

Along with being disingenuous salespeople, another thing you learn about Iranians is that we're incredibly nosy. I would get into the building's elevator and immediately the interrogations from the eighty-year-old neighbor women would commence.

"Are you Jobrani's son?"

"Yes ma'am."

"How much money does your fadder have?"

"Excuse me?"

"Is he vorth a million? Ten million? Vhat's your best guess?"

"I don't know."

"I'll take dat as ten million. Does your modder have fake boobs?"

"Excuse me?"

"I'll take dat as a yes. Have you ever had an STD?"

"That's none of your business."

"I'll take dat as a yes. How many people live in your house?"

"Are you with the census?"

"No, I'm just Persian."

It was strange to live surrounded by so many Iranians. Growing up, most of my friends were white, so I had been the most Iranian kid on the block. In Los Angeles, suddenly I was inferior. The Iranians of LA were so entrenched in their culture that some of them didn't even speak any English. I spoke Persian, but sometimes I would run into older Iranians who would use a word I didn't understand. I've learned in life that if someone uses a word you don't comprehend, you just need to nod confidently and agree: "I know exactly what you mean, my friend."

In the 1990s in Los Angeles, one of the people I dealt with on a daily basis who spoke little English was my grandfather. He came to America in the eighties to live with us in Marin. When the family moved to Los Angeles, we packed him in the truck with the rest of our stuff. For him, it was as if he'd returned to Tehran, since everyone in Westwood spoke Persian and he could just walk around visiting families and spend hours reciting poetry with other old Iranians. He was between eighty and ninety years old. I give a range because we really didn't know how old he was, nor did he. If you were born in Iran in the early 1900s and moved to America, you tended to lose track of your birth certificate. Not only did we not know how old he was, we didn't know his birthday. We would just throw him into the mix every once in a while when it was another family member's birthday. Often, he would end up having four or five birthdays a year, which is how he lived to be 273.

Grandpa was a great source of inspiration to all of us. He was retired but somehow kept himself busy each day. He awoke early and, like an old-timey gentleman, put on his three-piece suit and fedora hat. He would take the local bus to Santa Monica, where he would go shopping at the farmer's market. He knew everyone and everyone knew him. He had Iranian friends, American friends, even Mexican friends. My sister and I followed him once to see what he did all day, sort of like a ride-along day with grandpa. He would get to the market and greet the Mexican guys selling oranges. They would greet him in Spanish and Grandpa would respond in Persian. Somehow they both knew what the other was saying, a mishmash of greetings that seemed to work. Grandpa would then come home, cook for the entire family, and clean all the dishes at the end of the night. In between all of his work he would read books and listen to the Persian radio. He was as busy as Ryan Seacrest—and 240 years older.

Grandpa also had a potty mouth, and not just any potty mouth. The man was a blasphemy artist. When he got worked up, he could spew such beautiful and ornate profanity, it was like watching Michelangelo paint. Older Persians living in the United States love to listen to Persian radio. For our family it was a great way to keep Grandpa informed of what was going on in the old country, but it also got him angry. He was a big critic of the Iranian regime and sometimes, as he was listening to a debate about the Iranian government and their human rights abuses, he would lose it. One moment, he was this gentle, proper, fedora-wearing poet. The next he would cuss out the regime, spewing crass words and spitting. You'd be in the other room and suddenly hear, "May a cow make love to the dead grandmothers of these Iranian politicians!"

I'd run toward the violence. "Grandpa, are you okay?"

"I'm okay, but this shitty government suppressing the people is not! I hope the entire regime gets molested by a herd of fishhook-cocked goats infested with herpes!"

And the worst part—as a good Persian grandson, I still had to give this man a good-night kiss. On the mouth.

The Community Will Talk

When I first moved to Los Angeles, I was in limbo in regards to my career. I had applied to Ph.D. programs in political science at universities around the country and was waiting for the results. At the time, my father was living in Iran and my mother was in L.A.

raising my two younger brothers. With my father gone, it was decided that I would be the man of the house. This is something you see in immigrant cultures, where the eldest son is expected to take over the duties of the father if the father is not around. For example, in 1941, the shah of Iran took over the throne when his father was sent into exile. He was only twenty-one. Unlike the United States, where we have a presidential election with numerous backup plans, Iran had a monarchy with a simple "man of the house" plan. Except with the shah it was more "man of the country." Point being that immigrants expect the eldest son to run the family as soon as the father is out of the picture. If the eldest son leaves as well, then the next son takes over. If the next in line is a daughter, she has to get a sex change or at least dress in a suit. Persians take "man of the house" seriously.

My father moved to Iran in the early nineties for business. Being Iranian, he and my mom never spoke of separating or getting a divorce. I guess they figured that the law would eventually figure out that they really weren't into each other anymore and automatically issue them an international divorce. This became a big deal years later when my mom, who finally came to her senses, officially filed for divorce in the United States. When my father found out he was livid. He had been away from her for years and admittedly had no romantic feelings, but he still could not believe she would do such a thing.

"How could she divorce me?"

"Dad, you haven't seen her in eight years."

"Dat's true, but I vas vorking on a poem for her. Dese tings take time."

"You were living with another woman in another country."

"Don't change deh subject. Your modder is very unge-rateful."

"And also very realistic."

"People in deh community," he said, "vill talk." Which was the main reason for his anger.

I've never figured out who these people are, but I do know that Iranians live in fear of being judged by other Iranians. Anytime your parents don't want you to do something, they automatically pull the "community card."

"Don't be a comedian, deh community vill talk."

"Don't date be-lack people, deh community vill talk."

"Don't be gay, deh community vill talk."

"And vhatever you do, don't be a gay, be-lack comedian. Deh community vill be very confused."

When you're a kid and your parents guilt you with talk of the community, it really makes you upset. Like you're letting down 2,500 years of Persians and their history. The weight of the whole Persian Empire rests on your shoulders when the community speaks. You walk down the streets in Westwood and you think everyone is aware that you've chosen to become a comedian. To Iranians, the only occupation worse than a comedian is terrorist. You can swear they're shaking their heads in disgust. "Did you hear about Jobrani's son? He became a comedian. Yes, a kelown. A circus kelown. Dis vill ruin deh reputation of Persians all over deh vorld. Ve had an empire. Now ve have a kelown!"

With my father the poet in exile in Iran, and my grandfather the poet cursing at the radio at night, I was now the man of the house and faced with a major dilemma. I received a letter from New York University offering me a scholarship to earn my Ph.D. NYU would pay for all my education and give me a stipend as well. It wasn't the top university for political science, but it was a very good school. The advantage of going to NYU over UCLA, which I had also gotten into and was a better school, was that my education costs would be covered. You'd think that your parent would be happy to hear such good news. When I told my mother she began to cry.

"Vhy you go to New York? Your fadder leave me and now you leave."

"I thought you didn't like him?"

"Dat's not deh point. You are man of deh house. You must eh-stay."

"I'm only twenty-one."

"Deh shah ran a country at your age."

"His father was a dictator."

"And yours vasn't?"

"Leave Dad out of it."

Leaning in for the kill, she whispered, "People in deh community vill talk!"

Man of the House

The guilt worked. In the back of my head was this tiny voice reminding me that what I really wanted to do was comedy. Had I gone to New York, I would've been far away from home and might have had the guts to give it a try. But my mom pulled her Jedi community trick and I gave in. I decided to attend UCLA and live at home to be the man of the house. When you accept such a weighty role, you soon realize that the reality doesn't live up to the title. Whereas the shah got to run a country with ministers and generals and armies, and possible access to all the unmarried women in the land, I got to help my mother read her mail, drive my brothers to school, and help Grandpa with the English pronunciation of his cursing. I was more of a chauffeur/butler/profanity coach, a.k.a. a utility player.

Once in a while I got other man of the house duties, when my mom would make me sit my brothers down and talk to them. My father's departure left a void of male energy in the house, so my two younger brothers had run a bit rampant, putting my mom through hell in the process. Now, as the man, I had to fix the problem and get the boys back on track. Being an older brother and trying to act like a father did not go smoothly. Especially since my younger brothers had grown up in America, on the American hormone-infested diet of Big Macs, Whoppers, and Twinkies, which made them bigger than me. It isn't only the fries that get super sized—it's also the immigrants. I would sit them down and do my best, giving them fatherly advice, but it never sunk in, mostly because the "when I was your age" speech isn't as effective when you were their age only five years earlier. Real fathers told their sons about fighting in Vietnam or World War II. My war stories were much more passive.

"You should be grateful," I'd holler at my indifferent brothers. "When I was your age we had the Falklands War. It lasted seventy-four days and I wasn't even there. Then, of course, the invasion of Grenada. That lasted at least two weeks and I had to watch it on *Nightline* with Ted Koppel and his big hair. Every. Single. Night."

Screw the Ph.D.

I wasn't scaring anyone straight. Man of the house by night, Ph.D. student by day, I had delusions of grandeur. I had studied abroad in Italy my junior year as an undergrad and met a professor who inspired me toward academia. His name was Vincenzo Pace, but he went by Enzo. He had a goatee and would wear professorial blazers with elbow patches to class. He also had a gold pocket watch that he would pull out every day and look at as the last few ticks counted down to the beginning of class. Then he would flip the watch closed, put it back in his pocket, and very dramatically hold his hands in the sky in a pensive way, calling out the subject of the day in Italian.

"*Allora . . . Maometto.*" Which meant, "So . . . Mohammad."

This was a sociology of religion class. We would discuss the prophet Mohammad or Jesus or Moses and their philosophies. Something about the way he carried himself, how he spoke about these deep ideologies, made me believe that being a professor was exactly the vocation for which I'd been searching. On the one hand, it would make my mom happy because it would be an honorable profession that the community would look upon favorably. On the other hand, it would place me at a university where I could discuss ideas and debate with like-minded people, a modern-day prophet of sorts. Plus, I would be surrounded by young coeds the rest of my life. What prophet doesn't want that? It was all coming together splendidly—until I started studying for the actual Ph.D.

One thing you never hear about in the prophet business—it takes a shitload of studying to get a handle on all those complicated philosophies and theories. I remember getting into my Ph.D. classes at UCLA and discussing what our purpose was in the practical world as academics. The professor kept telling us that our goal in life would be to publish or perish. So basically we had to keep writing books on our theories and go around the world defending ourselves. If we were lucky enough to come up with a theory that a politician actually liked, then we might get to apply our ideas to the real world. In essence, we were living in a theoretical world, but every month when I got my tuition bill it didn't feel theoretical at all. Eight thousand dollars a year so that I could live in a theoretical world? At least they gave us student identification cards which got us two-dollar discounts at the movie theaters in Westwood. I figured if I saw four thousand films I would break even. In theory I had come up with a solution that was brilliant. In reality, I was an idiot.

I wasn't happy, either as the man of the house or a prophet in training. Something was missing. Eventually I dropped out of UCLA and began working at an advertising agency. I had to do something in an office just to get my mother off my back. I figured if she saw me going to work in a tie every morning, she would think I was doing something useful.

"You are not a lawyer, but at least you look like von!"

The first day on the job, the others in the agency told me to lose the tie. "We're much more laid-back here, so just dress casually."

When I told my mom, she almost rescinded my man of the house duties. "Casual? Vhat the hell does dat mean? It is an office. People vear ties in an office. You tell dose Americans dere is notting casual about vork. You are supposed to be uncomfortable at vork, from vhat you do to vhat you vear. I swear if it vere not for dis regime I vould move you back to Iran and make you vear a tie."

"Mom, they've banned ties in Iran."

"Den you vear a turban. Anyting to make you uncomfortable!"

A few months earlier I had seen Roberto Benigni receive the Grand Prix award for *Life Is Beautiful* at the Cannes Film Festival. I had become a fan of Benigni from my year in Italy. Seeing him win the award and rush the stage to kiss all the judges as well as Martin Scorsese's feet (who was the president of the festival—Scorsese, not his feet) inspired me. I remember thinking, *I want to be THAT excited about what I do in my life.*

One day I was dubbing a video copy of a play I had performed in and there was an older man who worked at the agency who saw bits of my play. He was a producer at the ad agency, named Joe Rein. Joe had always been complimentary to people and was one of those gems you meet in life. Watching me dub the play, Joe asked me if I had ever thought of pursuing acting professionally. I told him it had crossed my mind and that I was hoping to save money and pursue it when I turned thirty.

He took me into his office. "Look," he said, "I'm in my sixties. When I was in my twenties there were some things I really wanted to do. I kept putting them off and never got to them. So if you really want to do it, then do it."

It was the light bulb moment I had been waiting for. I realized that you live once and you cannot live the life your parents expect of you. All those years of struggling with my Persian identity and the obligations I had to my parents and the community had finally been revealed as futile. From that moment, I decided to prioritize acting and stand-up. Now there was only one last obstacle. In hindsight, a rather monstrous one. I had to tell my mother.

"Deh acting crap again?"

"Not just acting. Acting AND comedy."

"So da man of da house vants to tell jokes?"

"It's my passion, Mom."

"Your passion should be to make your modder happy."

"We're not in the old country. In America you're supposed to pursue your dreams."

"Okay, den I vould like to pursue my dereams, too. My deream is dat you go to law eh-school, get your degree, get a good job, and buy your mother a car. Preferably a top-of-the-line black 401(k) Mercedes, vith leather seats. Or ve can vait till next year and you get me a 402(k). Something to make the community talk."

Los Angeles had gone to her head.

Part Two

Stand-Up and Pat-Downs:
Life on the Road

Hollywood, California

Comedy didn't just begin the day I had the light bulb moment at the advertising job. It was something I had been subconsciously pursuing since I was a teenager. I've developed a basic philosophy throughout my acting and comedy life that applies to everyone, regardless of one's career or passion: You're either inspired by greatness or you're inspired by mediocrity. One of those two extremes is what throws everyone into pursuit of his dreams. Meaning, you either see something that is so great and inspiring that you leap into action and attempt to replicate it. Or you see something so mediocre and pathetic that you immediately think, *Look at that sad bastard. I can do better.*

Take fire, as an example. Some younger readers might believe that fire came about when the iPhone created the lighter app for use at concerts, but I've got a different theory. Fire came about either when a caveman saw a fellow cave dweller successfully light fire and then get laid by all the hottest, hairiest cavewomen that same evening, or it came about when the same guy saw a fellow cave dweller rub some rocks together and explode in flames and said, "Well, I can't do any worse than that."

My inspiration came in both forms. Yes, the greatness/ mediocrity principle is not a mutually exclusive principle and is not a zero sum theory. It can be simultaneously applied as a paradigm and, when looked at as a bell curve, the greatness factor has an inverse relationship to the mediocrity factor. If you have no idea what I just said don't worry because neither do I. It's just something I picked up in my three months in the Ph.D. program at UCLA and I figured I might as well use some of that language since I spent eight grand acquiring it. I dropped out of academia and with that abandoned my dreams of being a learned prophet. I let down Professor Enzo, my mother, and the entire Westwood condominium community. But there was another mentor I'd always looked up to, and I intended to do right by him.

The Persian Eddie Murphy

I got into comedy because I was inspired by greatness—that of my earliest influence, Eddie Murphy. Growing up I was a big fan of Eddie on *Saturday Night Live*. His comedy was ingenious and he was everything I aspired to be. I had his albums at home and Eddie even taught me and my six-year-old brother how to cuss. We would go around the house practicing: "Goddamned, motherfucker, punk-ass son of a bitch!" Our parents, being immigrants, had no idea what we were talking about. "Dere English is getting good! Dey are using multisyllabic vords. And complete sentences! Who says American public eh-schools are bad?"

I studied all of Eddie's sets and TV appearances, and I decided that I was going to make it as a comedian, only younger and better and edgier. My first opportunity to give it a shot was at age seventeen, the peak of my sexual perversity. There was a high school talent show that was looking for acts. I had no discipline and no game plan, and my comedy back then was solely sexual in nature. Things like, "Why are genitalia located in the least agile parts of the body? Wouldn't they be more accessible if they were on the hand? Then you could go around having sex all day simply by high-fiving each other." I would write it down and think, *Wow, this is brilliant stuff, I'm on my way!* The next day I'd read what I'd written and have second thoughts: *This is total horseshit. Who the hell wrote this?* I was only a teenager and I had no idea how stand-up worked. I had yet to learn it takes years of writing and honing and trying out stuff for it to become good material. Given my lack of confidence, I chickened out of performing at that event, and it turned out to be a good decision. When I showed up to watch the other performers, I saw that the audience was made up of juvenile delinquents from a nearby prison. Somehow the organizers had neglected to relay that small detail. I counted my blessings. The last thing I needed for my comedy career was to be shanked at my first performance. Talk about a discouraging start.

As inspired as I was by Eddie Murphy, I still did not have the courage to do stand-up onstage. I'd been in a lot of school plays up until then. But with acting, there are writers, directors, other actors, the orchestra—an entire army of folks to blame if things go wrong. With stand-up, there's only one person to blame, and I was not confident enough to risk it. In college, I had no more confidence. I had taken a few acting classes and attended some shows. I remember wandering into a bar, and they were having this stand-up comedy competition for National Lampoon, which was looking for the funniest unknown comedian in America. There were only two guys in the competition, and they were onstage doing their thing. They were both awful. I sat there thinking I could have climbed onstage right then, without any practice, and done a better comedy set than either of them. And boom—just like that, based on witnessing utter mediocrity, I told myself that the next time an opportunity to perform came around, I would take it.

One day I was listening to the biggest hip-hop radio station in the Bay Area and they announced that they were hosting a Dirty Dozens comedy competition for local comics. I had no idea what Dirty Dozens was, but I figured it meant there would be twelve people competing and maybe they wouldn't have to shower before the show. It was open to anyone, and even though I still had not performed stand-up comedy onstage, in my mind I was the next Eddie Murphy and funnier at least than the two guys I had seen bomb in the bar. I had a buddy record a video of me doing character impersonations and I sent it in. There were more than one thousand submissions, and I was one of sixteen finalists selected to go down to the radio station to promote the competition that would take place in front of thousands of people in a theater in Oakland. I put on my best outfit, strutted down to the studio, and prepared to take my place among the comedy greats. After a few moments, I realized my mistake: Dirty Dozens meant a "yo mama" comedy competition. While it was very Eddie Murphy in nature, I did not yet have the chops to hang with those guys.

All the other comics were black. And they knew one another from the comedy circuit, whereas I had never performed stand-up. Paranoia set in quickly. I decided they had not chosen me because my act was tight; they chose me to be the dude who everyone would laugh at and boo offstage, like they do on *American Idol* or *Showtime at the Apollo*. They were laughing at me, not with me.

But I couldn't just leave, and I had made a promise to myself that I was going to try. We were shuffled into the deejay's studio, and the other comedians were going around the room doing their best yo mama jokes directed at one another.

"Suki's mama so fat she can't wear a Malcolm X T-shirt because helicopters try to land on her."

"Coco's mama so ugly, she make blind children cry."

"Yo mama so fat people jog around her for exercise."

I just sat in the corner in silence, thinking, *Oh god, please don't let them notice me.* I don't have any yo mama jokes. And if my mother found out someone insulted her on the radio and I didn't defend her honor, she would never let me hear the end of it.

"You let dem call me fat? On deh radio? And you didn't beat dem vith a hanger? You are a disgrace to deh Jobrani name and deh entire Persian community."

I was sweating, panicking. I had no idea what to say when it was my turn. I was scared to do a yo mama joke because black guys take their mamas seriously. Back in California in those days, you could get killed for insulting someone's mama, especially if the yo mama joke hit too close to home. Finally after what felt like an hour of yo mama jokes, but was actually about two minutes, the deejay asked all the comics in the room to introduce themselves. They had gotten to the part of the show where I could participate. After all, I did know my own name. I listened as they all gave some cool shout-outs to their friends—"This is Suki from Viejo, shout-out to Pookey. You gonna be out of prison soon, homey!" "What-up, this is Coco from Oakland. Shout-out to the good Lord!"

Finally it was my turn. I'm not sure what happened, but

suddenly I transformed into a black comic: "Yo yo yo! What's up WHAT'S UP?! This is Mazzy J, sayin' what's up?"

Mazzy J? Who the hell was Mazzy J? And how many times was I going to say, "What's up?" I left the radio station feeling less funny, but more black, which was an interesting trade-off.

Fortunately for me, the promoter had a hard time selling tickets for this show, and it was canceled. Again, the comedy gods had smiled upon me by taking me out of a situation in which I would have been scarred for life. I dodged getting shanked once, and now I was dodging getting booed offstage at a black comedy competition.

I Used to Wash Toilets

My comedy dreams took some time to marinate, about five years. A fresh dropout from UCLA working the advertising gig, I decided I had to get serious about this comedy thing, so I enrolled in a stand-up class. The first thing they teach you is to write what you know and what makes you unique. In a class filled with guys, girls, straight people, gay people, short people, tall people, Asians, and even an Arab, I was the only Iranian. I'm guessing that's because most other Iranians were in law school or medical school, making their mothers happy and my mother jealous. The teacher told me to write about the struggles of being Iranian in America. This was easy, because Iranians had been vilified for so long. They say comedy comes from tragedy, and being Iranian in America from 1979 on had been quite tragic. I'd had some struggles myself, but in stand-up comedy I was able to take the reality and exaggerate it. Sometimes it would come across a bit cheesy, but the audience still laughed. Some of my earliest material was about my family life and how difficult it was to invite other kids over to spend the night because their parents were concerned we were going to take the kids hostage. I know, rimshot. But it worked.

We honed our material over the course of seven weeks and ended with a showcase at the Melrose Improv, where we were told big-time managers and agents would be in the audience to discover us and send us on the road to fame. A lot of acting and comedy classes in Los Angeles use these showcases to lure students in and get you to pay five hundred dollars to train with them. You're actually convinced that after less than two months of doing stand-up, someone will see you and put you on *Saturday Night Live*. The reality is much different. Now that I've been a stand-up for seventeen years, I know there is never one big night when everything comes together. It is a series of big nights and many years of hard work that, if you're lucky, will eventually pay off. If you ever take an acting or comedy class and after only two months a big agent wants to sign you, chances are he's trying to get in your pants. The night of my big showcase, there were no agents or managers, but someone much more important did attend: my mother.

I was a bit wary, because my mother had attended a play I had done a few years before called *Belind Date*. (Basically *Blind Date*, said with a Persian accent.) It was a comedy about a Persian guy who's a big bullshit artist and who goes on a blind date with a Persian girl who's a gold digger. It turned out to be a huge hit. At the time I was still living at home with my mom and I needed the ego boost. I came offstage and people were congratulating me and buying me drinks. I was getting a big head as I waved and shook hands with my hordes of new fans. I found my mom and escorted her to the valet line so that she could get her car and head home. Even as we waited in line, people congratulated me and I thought that she would finally realize what a star I was. That's when my mom chimed in.

"You vere good."

"Thanks, Mom."

She got in her car and started to drive off, but not before pulling down her window and blurting out one last thing.

"Just remember, funny man, dat tomorrow is your turn to vash the bathrooms."

This was said loud enough so that my fans could hear, bringing me back down to Earth. Head back to normal. Mission accomplished.

So when my mother appeared at the stand-up comedy showcase it made me nervous. I knew how high her standards were. If it didn't go well, she would never let me hear the end of it. Even if it went well, she would probably still embarrass me in front of everyone: "You did a good job, Maz. Next time make joke about how you vet your bed until you vere ten." This woman had a lot of secrets on me. I had to be careful when I took her out in public.

In a show with a bunch of lousy amateurs, I succeeded in being one of the better lousy amateurs. Afterwards, as people congratulated me, again I found my mom and braced myself for her to blurt out an inappropriate comment.

"You vere good!"

"And?"

"And vhat?"

"Aren't you going to say something to deflate the compliment?"

"I vould never do dat!"

"Last time you reminded me it was my turn to clean the bathroom."

"Dat vas just fact! Vhy you so sensitive?"

"I don't know. Maybe I have mother issues."

"Or maybe you're just a pussy."

Gigging in Strip Clubs

People ask me all the time how to become a stand-up comedian. The answer is simple: Get onstage as much as you can and write as much as you can. This sounds easier than it is because if you're not committed it's easy to be discouraged. I have done gigs in coffee shops where no one is listening and the barista decides to make the foam for the cappuccino right as you hit your punch line. I've done shows in church basements with only eight audience members, all of whom were there to perform their own variety acts as soon as I finished. The most bizarre show I ever did was in a strip club, where the club owners had sold the place the night before and taken the microphone with them.

The show was at a place called Treasure Island, the treasure being scantily clad girls dancing on greasy poles. The booker was a guy who did old-school jokes like you might hear in the vaudeville days. "Take my wife . . . please!" This guy booked the room so that he could get himself stage time on a weekly basis and work on his jokes, which were atrocious. (This is a common occurrence—guys who no one else will book deciding to get their own venue.) I was new to stand-up, so I took any gig I could get. Truth be told, I was quite atrocious myself.

The guy told me he would pay me five bucks for every audience member I brought. I was excited that this would be my first paid gig, but I didn't want to overpromote because I wasn't ready to perform in front of a large crowd. I told a few friends and asked them to keep it a secret. The opposite happened. In a room with thirty-eight audience members, thirty-one had come to see me. That meant I would make $155 that night, but also that I would bomb in front of enough people to get the word out to the community that I stunk. Furthermore, it wasn't until I showed up at the venue that I was told that the microphone was missing. It was decided that the show must go on and we would just shout our stand-up at the crowd.

If you've never done stand-up in a strip club, don't. People who go to strip clubs are not there to laugh. Some might giggle depending on how the girl dances on their laps, but laughter is not the main motivation. We quickly discovered that this was the worst location for a stand-up show when one of the patrons from the main room walked into our back room, stripper in tow. This gentleman, dressed as a gangbanger and looking quite dangerous, proceeded to sit in the center of the room where our microphone-less show took place. He held a loud conversation with the stripper, who was sitting on his lap. The guy didn't seem to care that there was a desperate comedian onstage shouting horrible jokes so everyone could hear. At one point the comic couldn't ignore his chatter any longer.

"Sir, I'm telling jokes up here. Can you keep it down?"

"You talking to me?"

"Yes, I'm talking to you. Keep it down."

"Mind your own business, asshole!"

The poor comedian looked to the rest of us for help—other comedians, the organizer, even the audience—but no one said a word. The guy had a stripper on his lap, and he seemed to be totally comfortable with telling the comic onstage to mind his own business. From the way he was dressed, we were certain this guy was capable of busting a cap in somebody's ass.

A few of the people I had invited were shooting me stink eyes—what kind of a place had I invited them to? I shrugged. A typical selfish comedian, I was just relieved that this wasn't happening during my set. Fortunately, the booker had scheduled me last to hold my audience hostage and have them watch all the other comics. I guess he figured we Persians had held Americans hostage for 444 days, so he could at least hold a bunch of Persians hostage for two hours. It only seemed fair. By the time I got up I looked out at the audience and saw a bunch of familiar faces bored to death and kicking themselves for having come out to see me.

"I told you guys not to come," I wanted to holler. "It's not my fault you can't keep a secret." It was all I could do to shout my jokes so that those sitting in the rear could hear. And I was working faster than I wanted to, just in case the gangbanger brought another stripper in for a second conversation. When I finished, my friends rushed out quickly, issuing me polite smiles of pity. Some of them still haven't come back to see me perform. If any of you are reading this, please come back and give me one more shot. I promise—no strippers, no gangbangers, no bad jokes. But there's still a two-drink minimum.

Persian Blackface

The biggest break I got in my early stand-up career was becoming a regular at the Comedy Store. Being a regular means that you have performed in front of the owner of the club and she has approved you. It's a great honor and every struggling comedian wants to be a regular at all the big clubs. The Comedy Store in Los Angeles was, and is, one of the biggest clubs in the world. The owner, Mitzi Shore, who is Pauly Shore's mother, is a comedy legend. Her club has had a hand in developing the acts of Jay Leno, David Letterman, Robin Williams, Jim Carrey, Sam Kinison, Roseanne Barr, Andrew Dice Clay, and many more. It was the Comedy Store where Richard Pryor made a comeback later in his life and Eddie

Murphy would perform at the peak of his stand-up career. Even today you will see some of the hottest comedians stopping by to work out material. Sometimes it's Chris Rock, sometimes Dave Chappelle, Louis C.K.—the list goes on.

I first auditioned for Mitzi in 1999. At the time, a lot of my material was about being Iranian. There wasn't anyone else doing that material back then, so I stood out to her. After I performed three minutes one Sunday night, Mitzi told me to return the following week and do six minutes. I returned, did my six, and was told to return and do ten minutes. This was how you became a regular, with this painstakingly slow process that caused anxiety and crippling ulcers. Finally the day came for me to do my ten minutes in front of her. If I passed this obstacle I would be a regular.

Mitzi used to sit in the back seat next to the exit and watch the shows. If she liked you after your third audition she would grab your arm as you walked past, pull you in, and tell you that you were a regular. If she didn't like you, she would just ignore you as you passed. This was brutal. You wanted to make eye contact in the hope she would smile and pull you in, but you didn't want to make too much eye contact and seem presumptuous. You had to find a way to balance your anxiety for acceptance with a fake humility. It was like being in the fourth grade waiting to be picked for a kickball team. You hoped to hear your name but didn't want to seem too anxious in case your name was called last.

I did my ten minutes in front of Mitzi and it felt good. As I walked the thirty feet from the stage to the exit, I tried to act nonchalant. At the last moment, she reached out her hand and pulled me in. It felt like she waited for me to almost pass her just to mess with me a bit.

"You're very funny," she said.

"Thank you, Mitzi."

"I'm going to make you a regular."

It had happened. I had been chosen. By the guru herself. I was going to be a regular. Things were finally coming together. I wanted to celebrate, but I had to play it cool, as though I expected nothing less. "Thank you, Mitzi. I really appreciate it."

She pulled me closer. "Have you ever thought about wearing the outfit?"

"What outfit?"

"You know, the hat and robe."

"Hat and robe?"

"Yeah," she repeated, "the hat and robe."

I stared at her confused for a few seconds.

Then it hit me. She was asking if I had ever thought about wearing Middle Eastern garb, a turban and a dishdasha, onstage. I didn't know what to say. She was offering me a regular slot at the club where Eddie Murphy had performed, making one of my biggest dreams come true. But she was asking if I would dress as a sheikh or a mullah onstage. Was this racist? Was there a word for being both flattered and insulted at once?

"Well, I, uh, haven't really thought about it."

"Trust me," Mitzi said. "Wear the outfit."

The woman who held my career in her hands was basically presenting me with an ultimatum. If I wanted to perform in her club, I would have to don the Persian equivalent of blackface. This was outrageous. I could never do that to my people. I could never do that to my mother. It took only one second for me to make up my mind.

"That's brilliant, Mitzi! I will definitely wear the outfit. What a great idea! Thank you again for making me a regular."

I couldn't believe it as the words came out of my mouth. My conscience wanted to maintain integrity, but my soul—clearly looking for Hollywood stardom—sold out. I walked to the back parking lot and instead of celebrating, I paced and contemplated what had happened. I didn't want to perform in a costume. I would be the laughingstock of the club. My career would end before it even began. Then I had a thought. Mitzi was old. Old people forget things. Maybe by the time my next spot opened up, she would have forgotten about the whole idea.

The next day I called the club to give them my times for the week. The booker sounded very enthused to hear I was a regular.

"Maz, congratulations. I heard you passed."

"Yeah, I can't believe it."

"And she told me you're going to wear the outfit."

"Excuse me?"

"The hat and robe. It's a great idea."

"First of all, it's not a hat, it's a turban. Second, it's not a robe, it's a dishdasha." I grew irritated explaining this. "Third," I said with conviction, "I'm not wearing the outfit."

The air went out of the booker's enthusiasm. "If Mitzi wants you to wear the outfit, you should wear the outfit."

"What happens if I don't wear the outfit?"

"Do I really have to answer that?" She didn't. "Listen, if it makes you feel better, Mitzi is really good at these things. She's a visionary. She took Roseanne Barr shopping for her clothes to create her on-stage persona. She's done that with a lot of comics. If she thinks you should wear the outfit, it will be good for you. Trust me."

Mitzi hadn't forgotten. In fact, she was so behind this idea, it was the first thing she'd mentioned to the booker. I hung up, disappointed. I didn't think Mitzi had bad intentions, but I also didn't want to listen to her instincts in this case because I knew she was wrong. Then I came up with a plan. A few years earlier, there was an Iranian entertainer in the United States who would impersonate the mullahs on Persian TV. This guy would criticize the regime back in Iran. I guess the regime didn't find him too amusing because one time when he was performing live in Los Angeles someone showed up and threw a rock at him that hit him in the eye and made him go blind. I never researched this story, but that's what I had heard. And most importantly, that was the story I intended to stand by in order to raise a high alert at the Comedy Store. Armed with this information, I called the booker again.

"It's Maz," I said dramatically, quickly, out of breath. "I was working on the outfit when I just remembered something." I relayed the story of the possibly blind impersonator. "The last guy who wore *the outfit* ended up losing his sight because they threw rocks at him."

"Oh dear."

"And as much as I'm dying to wear the outfit, I would hate for it to get out that there's a guy at the Comedy Store impersonating mullahs and have them come blow the place up."

Silence on the other end. "Let me run this by Mitzi and see what she says." A few minutes later I got the call. "Maz, forget the outfit. Just wear something casual."

Thank God. Or should I say praise Allah.

Dying in Front of Eddie

I owe much of my success to Mitzi Shore and the Comedy Store. It was at this club where I was able to perform in front of small, drunk audiences night after night and grow exponentially as a comic. It was also Mitzi who launched my touring career. Because of Mitzi I was able to go on and do my own solo tours called "Brown and Friendly," "Browner and Friendlier," and "I Come in Peace," all of which would have been more interesting tour names had I still been performing in strip clubs. It was during my first solo tour when I would come face to face with my comedy hero of all time, Mister Motherfucker himself, Eddie Murphy.

I had been on the road in Australia doing hour-long sets. The shows were in front of hundreds, sometimes thousands, of people who had bought tickets to see me in concert. My dream of being like Eddie was coming true and I couldn't have been happier with my career. I had even managed to get my mom on board, and she was now one of my biggest fans. (For an Iranian, getting your mother off your back is the biggest measure of success in anything you do.) Life was beautiful.

On Tuesday nights the Comedy Store hosted black comedy night. The rumor was that Eddie Murphy occasionally hung out in the back to watch comedians perform. This was around the time when everyone was talking about when he was going to get back onstage and do his next comedy special, so there were always whispers when he was in the club that he was looking for inspiration. I was just back from Australia for a day, and rather than taking the night off and relaxing, I decided to go down to the club and do fifteen minutes to get a workout. For nearly a month I had been on the road, doing shows that were four times as long. Doing an hour show and doing a fifteen-minute show are very different beasts. They require completely different rhythms and timing, and it was just one of those late Tuesday nights, an empty audience, when my act was not as good as it should have been.

There were three rooms at the club—one was the Main Room,

which on Tuesdays hosted black comedy night. There was the Original Room, where I was performing, and the Belly Room, which has nothing to do with this story. Eddie Murphy was rumored to occasionally hang out in the back of the Main Room, but never in the Original Room, where comedians mostly worked out new material. What are the chances that a comic legend, and the one rock star performer who influenced my comedy from the beginning, would happen upon the workout room on the one night I was truly awful? Since I'm telling this story, the chances are pretty good.

I was having a bad set and the audience was quiet, maybe one guy in the room laughing. At one point I thought to myself that maybe I should do some older tried-and-true material to win the audience over. What if someone big was watching? Then I decided it didn't matter if someone big was watching. I had been doing shows in this room for years and not caring about who watched. That was the magic of the Original Room and why I had been able to grow as a comic—it made you not care about anything but working out your material. All these thoughts were running through my mind as I was doing my set. That night, I resolved to stick to my guns and not pander to the audience. If I was going to bomb, I would do it on my terms.

I came offstage. A comedy groupie who hung around the club came over and told me the news. "Hey Maz, Eddie's here tonight."

You know the person is important if you can refer to him by his first name and you instantly know who he is. Eddie is Eddie Murphy. Oprah is Oprah Winfrey. Michael is Michael Jordan, or Michael Jackson, or Michael J. Fox, or Michael Moore, or Michael Ian Black, or . . . okay, this theory doesn't necessarily work if your name is Michael.

Eddie Murphy had been sitting in the back of the room, listening to my set. My horrible, shitty, desperate set. I looked up and saw that he was occupying Mitzi's chair—the same one I had been so scared to walk by years before. The chair you have to walk by to exit the room. I took a deep breath and proceeded to walk in his direction. I tried to act nonchalant but was hoping he would grab my arm: "Hey kid, you weren't that bad tonight. Have you thought about wearing a turban?" Okay, I was hoping he wouldn't bring up the turban, but I wanted him to acknowledge me.

Unfortunately, he didn't pull a Mitzi. He let me walk right past. It really *had* been as bad as I thought. I walked down the steps and into the Comedy Store hallway, where I had to wait for my friend Anthony to come out so we could leave. When who walked out but my idol, Eddie himself. I stood there, hoping he might say hello, or offer me a handshake. Nothing. He gave me a quick look and then averted his eyes. He couldn't even bear the sight of me.

Suddenly those two mediocre comics who bombed in that bar almost twenty years earlier, way back at UC Berkeley, and made me believe I could do better, came rushing back. What if I had become that mediocre act for Eddie? I saw him making a comeback and going on a late night talk show to announce his return. At some point Jimmy Kimmel would lean over: "So, Eddie, what inspired you to come back?"

"Well, Jimmy, I was inspired by mediocrity. One night I saw this horrible Iranian comedian perform and I told myself right then—I can do better. He was awful. He didn't even wear a turban."

Washington, D.C.

The first time I visited Washington, D.C., to perform was with the Arabian Knights. That's not an all-male Middle Eastern stripper revue. It was the name of the Axis of Evil Comedy Tour before we changed the name. "Arabian Knights" was a name given to us by Mitzi Shore, who had put us together in the first place because she'd had the epiphany that there would be a need for a positive voice for Middle Eastern people in the near future. She had this epiphany before the September 11 attacks, but given how often you saw Middle Easterners get killed in Chuck Norris and Steven Seagal movies even then, it wasn't hard to deduce that we had replaced the Russians as the bad guys in the West. Ever since Rocky Balboa knocked out Ivan Drago in *Rocky IV* and he gave the speech to the Russian audience after the fight—"If I's can change, and you's can change, everybody can change!"—the Russian reputation has been on the upswing. Unfortunately, our reputation has plummeted. Mustafa has replaced Yuri because someone has to be the bad guy.

We showed up in D.C. to perform in the middle of the week and the place was packed. I had no idea that we would do so well, but it turned out that there were a lot of Middle Easterners and Muslims, as well as other liberal-minded people, who were sick of seeing us portrayed only as the bad guys and curious to see how we would do as entertainers. It seemed there had already been a fan base that was waiting for us to appear. We were filling a void, and the shows got bigger and hotter every time we returned. D.C. proved that Middle Eastern people aren't simply interested in kidnapping Americans; sometimes we like to make them laugh as well. (But when we do kidnap Americans, we are quite serious about it and you shouldn't laugh.)

D.C. is one of the best cities in which to perform comedy. It has an international culture, and the people living there are very politically minded. Whereas in Los Angeles you might come across an actor who tells you he is preparing for a part in a film in which he plays an FBI agent, in D.C. you meet the actual FBI agent. You ask people what they do and they tell you they're with State (the State Department), the Agency (the CIA), the Feds (FBI), etc. I get excited and nervous at the same time—excited that they have such important careers protecting the country, nervous that they're protecting the country from people who look like me.

I start rambling. "Are you packing a gun? Have you ever overthrown a dictator? Do I seem suspicious to you? I feel suspicious. Wanna search me? If I were you, I would totally search me."

My Jewish Heckler

It was as an international man of comedy that I returned to D.C. in 2006 to do another Axis of Evil show at the Warner Theatre. It was our biggest show to date, in front of eighteen hundred people, a truly electrified crowd that was exciting to be a part of. In the middle of my set, I did a joke making fun of John Bolton. Not Michael Bolton, the balding guy with the ponytail who sings "When a Man Loves a Woman." I know there are probably a lot of jokes a comedian could make about Michael Bolton, but as a bald man myself, I have a degree of respect for a balding man who once sported a ponytail. That's badass. Rather my joke was about John Bolton, the former U.S. ambassador to the United Nations with the walrus mustache. If you are reading this and live in D.C., you probably already know who he is. If you live in Los Angeles, you're probably putting down this book, picking up your phone, and googling "Ambassador Mustache."

I had worked Bolton into my routine because he had gone on TV and said that the United States would not call for a cease-fire in an ongoing battle between Israel and Lebanon because he didn't think it would accomplish anything. This incensed me. There were people dying on both sides and everyone knew that if the United States called for a cease-fire, it might encourage the two sides to stop fighting and lives would be saved. I intended to save the day—with an admittedly half-assed joke where I made fun of his mustache. The joke fared well in front of the liberal D.C. crowd, where it was met with some applause and support. However, a few nights later I did the same joke at the Comedy Cellar in New York City in front of twenty people. It didn't go so well. New Yorkers take facial hair seriously.

First of all, I had gone from performing in front of a packed house on a Saturday night to performing in front of twenty people on a Tuesday. That's the life of a comedian. We get up wherever and whenever we can. And, in fact, those smaller crowds are where we work out new material. I've performed in coffee shops, strip clubs as mentioned, even Alcoholics Anonymous meetings. (Side note: If you're ever performing at an empty AA meeting, don't open with "Good to see everyone tonight. Finally, a comedy show without a two-drink minimum. Am I right?")

The Tuesday evening I tried out the Bolton joke at the Comedy Cellar, a young Jewish guy in the audience didn't have the same politics as me when it came to Israeli-Lebanese bomb hurling. How did I know he was Jewish, you ask? I believe the yarmulke on his head gave it away. The Bolton mustache joke met with a few laughs, but more importantly, my Jewish nemesis booed loudly.

I wasn't sure if I had heard him right. "Sir, are you booing peace?" I asked.

"You need to educate yourself," he told me. "You sound like an idiot."

Comedians expect to do their sets, for the most part, without interruptions. Typically a drunk person, or someone just talking too loudly, might cause a disturbance, but you point it out and the person quiets down. But when someone flat out tells you you're an idiot—in front of an audience, albeit of only twenty people—you have to acknowledge it. You've been shown up. It's called being heckled. It is your job, as a comedian, to bury that person, shame him, ruin what is left of his night, if not his life. You have to impart such a great comeback that the audience roars in laughter and comes back to your side, putting the heckler in his place.

When the guy told me I was an idiot, I came after him fierce. "No, sir, it is you who is the idiot!"

I know that's not the wittiest retort, but it got my point across. I was angry at this guy and wanted to debate him on the issue. However, I had a microphone in my hand and nineteen other people staring at me, waiting to see me thrash my heckler. I really didn't have time to get into a discussion about Middle Eastern politics. I just wanted to put him in his place, but my heckler was ready for me.

"YOU are an idiot, man!"

"No," I insisted, a stage veteran all the way, "you are!"

"I said it first. You are!"

"No, it's you!"

"You!"

"You! You! You!"

It quickly devolved into a fourth grade playground fight, two idiots unable to come up with a better comeback. He was angry. I was angry. The whole room was tense. It began to feel like this guy was going to rush the stage, or I was going to jump into the crowd.

It's important to remember: I was an Iranian guy after September 11, in an argument with a Jewish guy, in New York City of all places. If I jumped on top of this guy, there was a very real possibility I would end up with a one-way ticket to Guantanamo. Furthermore, I'm not the "jump on top of hecklers" type. I've only been in one real fight my entire life.

Back in my early twenties, my friend got into a fight with a much bigger guy outside a bar in San Francisco and I had to back him up. This was a preppy part of town, so it was a preppy fight. We were wearing dress shirts, J. Crew sweaters, and Top-Siders. The other guy was dressed in a tux. (I assume he was coming from a wedding. Or maybe he was a maître d'.) Either way, he picked a fight with my friend and I had to get ghetto on his ass—all the while making sure I didn't get any blood on my nice sweater. It really never comes out of that type of material. So while the big guy was on top of my friend punching him, I was kicking the guy from behind.

All those years of playing soccer finally paid off. Whereas real fighters train in karate or jujitsu, I only knew how to use what I had learned growing up in Marin County playing midfield for the Tiburon Sharks. The big difference, though, between fighting some random guy in the streets and playing soccer in an affluent neighborhood is that with soccer you get a halftime break where one of the team moms gives you orange wedges and Capri Suns. And that team mom was never my mom, because when you have a Middle Eastern mom you try to keep her as far away from the field as possible for fear that she might bring some kebabs and yogurt soda for halftime instead of oranges and Capri Suns. Yes, there's such a thing as yogurt soda; it tastes as bad as it sounds.

Anyway, the only fight I was ever in was this one with my friend, which did not have a halftime or snacks. We actually ended up winning the fight because the bigger guy got up, dusted himself off in front of a crowd that had gathered, and gave us a warning as he walked off. (Kind of like Matt Dillon at the end of *My Bodyguard* when the nerdy kid beats him up.) Even though my fight record is 1–0, I still am not a fan of fights. If you've ever seen a picture of me, you'll realize I don't have the right nose for fighting. It sticks out too far and is just begging to be broken. So ninety-nine times out of one hundred, I will deal with a fight by talking my way out of it. The other time I will turn and run like a gazelle.

I even have a comedy special called "I Come in Peace." If I

got into a fight in public with a heckler, who would ever buy that DVD again? So this guy and I were going back and forth in the Comedy Cellar and it was escalating. Suddenly, the host, Ardie Fuqua, an affable black comedian, jumped back onstage, took the microphone from me, and began telling both of us to calm down.

Now we have an Iranian, a Jew, and a black guy in a bar, the beginning of a solid joke. In reality, it was turning into a nightmare. Ardie was acting like a boxing referee, telling us both to go to our corners. He got us to agree that we would behave, then handed me the microphone. I had never had an experience like that before where it had gotten so bad the host had to relieve me of the microphone. Comedians are supposed to deal with their own hecklers. Getting another comedian involved made me feel like I wasn't seasoned enough to handle my own problems. To make it worse, it wasn't like he took the microphone and told me to leave the stage. He took it, played referee, and then handed it back to me. It was up to me to get the audience back in a fun mood. It was as if someone had a heart attack at a party, died, and once the medical personnel removed the body, the host said, "Okay everyone, let's not let one dead body ruin the party. Everyone get back to dancing!"

I was trying to set the show back on track and basically struggling to get some laughs. I was steaming, just really aggravated and wanting to debate—and possibly fist-fight—the Jewish heckler. A bouncer finally arrived and escorted the guy out of the club. Now all I could think of was getting offstage and taking this argument outside. But the heckler and I were not to meet again. The club management, rightfully, told me to chill upstairs with the other comedians after my set.

It wasn't until I was telling some of the other comics what had happened that I realized the irony of the situation. I set out to tell a joke that had a message of peace and human compassion and found myself willing to get into a fight over it. How did I get so worked up? Did things like this ever happen to my heroes of peace like Martin Luther King? Did Gandhi ever get heckled to the point where he wanted to take off his loincloth and slap someone with his sandals: "Turn your cheek so I can slap it, bitch!" Being peaceful isn't easy.

Getting heckled is a natural part of stand-up comedy. No matter what you say, someone is going to take it the wrong way and yell something at you at some point.

"Babies are adorable," you might say.

"Go fuck yourself," some angry comedy expert will inevitably holler. "And tell the babies to go fuck themselves, too."

Now, if this happened to you in a normal conversation you could take your time, look the person in the eye, and try to understand his point of view as to why the babies should, indeed, go fuck themselves. But when you're onstage and someone interrupts your set, you must react quickly.

Each comic has his own comeback. One might say, "How do you propose a baby with a baby penis goes and fucks itself?" I, on the other hand, would probably say, "Oh yeah? Oh yeah? I tell you what. You are an idiot!"

Friendly Nuclear Program

Things can get especially volatile when the subject turns to politics. This was the case when the George W. Bush administration took the country into war with Iraq. My relationship with Bush, Cheney & Co. seesawed in the early 2000s. When they won the election I was upset and called foul on the recount. However, when September 11 happened, I found myself supporting their call for justice. I even purchased an American flag and stuck it on my car. (Fine, that was mostly so people wouldn't mistake me for al-Qaeda and shoot me, but I also felt very patriotic.)

I remember loving Bush, listening to his speeches and eagerly hollering my approval. That's how patriotic I'd become: I loved George W. Bush and whatever he had to say. "USA! USA! USA damn it! Let's get them damn terrorists! Go Dubya!"

I remember when he coined the term "axis of evil." He was explaining how we needed to fight the terrorists. The terrorists from September 11 had been Saudis and Egyptians, so I figured he would mention something about reviewing our relationship with those two countries. Not that I wanted to attack them per se, but I figured if he's announcing an axis of evil, one of those countries was going to make the list. He named the axis.

Bush: "It's North Korea."

Me: "Didn't see that one coming, but okay, I can see how they're evil."

Bush: "Eye-rack."

Me: "Hmmm. Interesting choice, interesting choice. I wonder where he's going with this. Must be saving Egypt or Saudi Arabia for last."

Bush: "And Eye-ran."

Me: "Eye-what? Did he say Eye-ran? What the hell just happened?"

How did Eye-ran get into the axis? I'm Eye-ranian . . . I mean Iranian. I'm not evil. Okay, Iran does have a nuclear program. But it's a peaceful nuclear program. They might make a bomb, but they would only use it to deliver flowers and ice cream, probably to

Israel, the Great Satan, or any other infidel state that didn't believe in peace.

Like much of the country, I began questioning the administration's ulterior motives with Iraq. They were using September 11 for their political agenda, and I felt it was my duty, as a comedian, to bring this to light onstage. I would mention in my shows that after the September 11 attacks there had been an outpouring of support for the victims from around the world. There was even a candlelight vigil in the streets of Iran. It felt like the world had come together against terrorism. And yet, just a couple of years later, we had ignored that gesture of unity and decided to take a hawkish route toward war.

The whole thing was a big joke, with the United States organizing a "coalition of the willing" to attack Iraq. This was an attempt to show that the world was behind us in beginning this war. The willing included the United Kingdom, Australia, and Poland, all legitimate allies. But then it went on to include the Marshall Islands, Eritrea, and the Federated States of Micronesia. I think Eritrea sent five soldiers. And what the hell is the Federated States of Micronesia? That just sounds like a place where Asians brew beer.

I went on the offensive with my jokes, making fun of the war, but not everyone was on board. Quite often I would be in the middle of a set, doing a joke about Bush, and someone would tell me I couldn't make fun of the president. This happened once at the Comedy Store. A young girl sitting in the front row told me that she was in the military and that she took offense at my jokes about our commander in chief.

"We're at war. You can't make fun of the president."

"According to the administration, that's one of the main reasons we're at war: to bring democracy to Iraq," I told her. "And you're telling me that in our own country I should limit my freedom of speech because you disagree with me?"

"Yep."

"The reason I love the United States is because we CAN make fun of the president. That's what differentiates us from Iraq or Iran. If I were to make fun of the president of Iran in Iran, it's safe to say that would be my last show in Iran."

On the eve of the war with Iraq, the administration sold a line to the public that if you criticized the war, you were criticizing the troops. It was ridiculous, but people were hesitant to laugh at jokes about Bush or the war. I had to remind audiences that I wasn't making fun of the troops. You never hear a comedian say, "I love the administration. I love that Dick Cheney. It's those damn troops that piss me off." It was all pretty hairy. It was made even hairier because the words were coming out of the mouth of a Middle Easterner whose allegiance could be questioned. I had a few people walk out on me because they didn't like what I was saying. The war was being fought thousands of miles away, but the repercussions were being felt in comedy clubs around the country.

Old Women Heckle, Too

Heckling doesn't always take a political form. It runs the gamut. Stand-up comedy isn't exactly a gated community. Anyone with twenty bucks can get into a club, so the dregs of society can show up and ruin your set. I've even been heckled by old Persian women who have sat through an hour of my show waiting for me to tell jokes in Farsi. Why they are at my shows in the first place if they don't speak English is beyond me. I think what has happened is that people in the Persian community have heard my name, maybe seen a clip or two on YouTube, and they assume that when I perform live I will bust out all the Farsi jokes.

One night during a show, a woman in her sixties, dressed in furs, expensive jewelry, and clothing you would more likely see at an ambassador's ball than a comedy show, hollered, "Tell us some joke in Farsi!" When I explained I didn't do jokes in Farsi, she replied, "You should!" This all sounds innocent enough, but her tone had the subtext of, "You're not funny, maybe if you tried it in Farsi you'd be funny. You suck!"

As I've mentioned, when challenged by a heckler you have to be ready with a good comeback. So when a lady your mother's age, dressed in ballroom attire, heckles you, you have to be quick, but you must be sure it's not too cruel lest you force the crowd to sympathize with her.

"Ma'am, are you aware that there are five hundred other people watching the show in English and enjoying it?"

"Yes, but I am not. Tell a joke in Farsi."

"You are interrupting the show to make a personal request. I am not a jukebox. Don't you feel selfish?"

"No, I don't. I paid for my ticket. Now tell a joke in Farsi, Meester Jukebox."

After a show, these ladies occasionally approach me and speak in broken English.

"I am sorry if I make terouble. I not mean to haggle you."

"Haggle me?"

"My kids. Dey say I haggle you."

"You mean heckle."

"Heckle, haggle. Same ting. You know problem? You should tell joke in Farsi. Might make you funny!"

The irony is that haggling is what Middle Eastern people do

innately, and very well, at bazaars and department stores. I once had an aunt haggle with a salesclerk at a department store in Italy until the guy crumbled and gave her his own employee discount. The art of haggling is in our blood. Heckling, on the other hand, is not one of our more natural states. As a culture, Middle Eastern people are taught to be respectful and not to be too outspoken in public. Even if we do heckle, we do it in a coy way. Rather than shouting, "You suck!" a Middle Easterner might say, "I vonder if you've ever considered anodder career." Not as hard-hitting, but just as effective.

The Time Barack Touched My Wife

Washington, D.C., has always been good to me. I feel like I'm surrounded by like-minded people there. Part of the reason is that it's a pretty liberal place. Even during the Bush administration, when audiences around the country would get upset at Bush jokes, the folks in D.C. howled at them. All you had to do was mention his name and a thousand people would roar. I almost felt bad for the guy when he was living in D.C. and no one there seemed to respect him. Part of it was that the crowds I was attracting were opposed to the war. I'm sure there were a few covert FBI or CIA types monitoring my shows, and they were instructed to laugh in order to blend in. Some of those same guys might be reading this book right now, looking for clues to my involvement with jihad. Let me save you the trouble, guys, and tell you that I gave up on jihad a long time ago. First, when I heard about the size of beard you had to grow to fight for Allah, I stopped going to weekly jihad meetings. Then I just lost interest altogether once I learned they were putting bombs in their underwear.

D.C. is also a great place because sometimes you see these big leaders you're used to seeing on TV out and about and you're reminded that they, too, are human. I remember after September 11, Bush appointed Tom Ridge as the secretary of Homeland Security. If you don't remember Tom Ridge, he was a big guy with a flat nose that looked like he'd been a boxer or a football player. He was basically Sheriff Number One in the country fighting terrorism, and he seemed like a pretty serious badass. I remember seeing him one night outside a fancy restaurant talking to a young lady. I thought, *Holy shit! This guy wants to get laid, too? Shouldn't he be looking for Osama? How does he have time to flirt? If another attack happens it could be because he was trying to get lucky with a girl half his age.* This guy was the secretary of Homeland Security. Can you imagine the pickup lines?

"You must be al-Qaeda. One look at you and my alert level goes up."

"You've been randomly selected. For a Big Tom cavity search."

One of my coolest trips to D.C. was when I got invited to the Obama White House for a Christmas party. When you get an invite from the White House and you're not a world leader or an ambassador, you think it's most likely junk mail requesting a donation. But my wife inspected it and it was legitimate. I couldn't believe it. I had no idea why I was being invited. Being the paranoid Middle Easterner that I am, I thought maybe it was a ploy to get me there and arrest me for something I must have done, or was about to do. Or maybe it was an attempt to turn me into a spy for the administration. Either way, I was going to D.C. to hobnob with the president and first lady, sugarplums and delusions of grandeur dancing in my head.

An interesting thing I learned about being invited to the White House: Everyone in your life will suddenly have a very important message for you to deliver to the president. One friend, a Democrat, told me to ask the president to raise taxes. My Republican friend asked me to tell him to cut taxes. My mom reminded me she doesn't pay taxes because she buys everything in cash, but to tell Obama that she loved him.

That's a characteristic of a lot of immigrants and definitely of Middle Easterners—we like to deal in cash and we keep it in secret accounts, or under our beds, or in the walls. That way, no one knows how much you have, and you're ready to escape in case a revolution occurs. My grandmother used to keep all her money in her bra. We thought she was a D cup until we went to buy a house and she pulled the down payment out of her bra, revealing that she was only an A cup.

I had no idea what the party would be like, but as the messages piled up I thought I would have to corner the president for a good hour to relay all the missives from my friends, family, and neighbors.

When my wife and I arrived, we learned this was one of many Christmas parties the White House would be having during the holiday season. We also discovered we would only meet the president and first lady for five seconds total. Just long enough to take a picture and have me tell the president to raise taxes, then to reduce taxes, then that my mom doesn't pay taxes but she loves him, and with the leftover time tell him all about my grandmother's bra bank. Time was limited so I just ended up telling him my mother loved him. At least I delivered one crucial message.

The best part of going to the White House was that it was a great date night for my wife and me. We had been in the trenches with our kids for a while and it gave us an evening to get away. There's no better way to impress your wife than to tell her you're taking her to a party at the house of the most powerful man in the world. Most of the night we just walked around eating free food and taking pictures with paintings of former presidents. As if to say, "We never met the real person, but we did once stand next to an image of him."

My wife worried that the pictures we took with the Obamas had not come out well. She claimed that when the cameraman told us to look, the president had put his arm around her waist, making her turn to him and not look at the camera.

"Whoa, whoa, whoa. What do you mean he put his arm around your waist? You mean flirtatiously?"

"I just felt him pull me in tight so I looked at him."

"Pull you in tight? Who does he think he is? The president of the United States?"

"I'm just saying that it messed up my picture concentration."

"You want me to go back and ask them to take another picture?"

"No!"

"I'd like to go back and ask him why he put his arm around your waist."

"Are you crazy?"

"I can't believe he touched you like that. What about me? I'm the one who got us the invite! The least he could've done was put his arm around both our waists. You know how many years I've been coming to D.C. to perform? You have any idea how many times I've had to deal with hecklers, defending this guy's politics? I just want to be held."

Denver, Colorado

Shortly after the September 11 terrorist attacks, I was carrying a duffel bag through an airport on my way to a gig. It was a tense time in the world—not just for Middle Easterners like me, who because of my ethnicity might merit a more intimate pat-down by burly TSA guards, but also for regular folks worried that the al-Qaeda-looking hoodlum—that would be me—was stowing some sort of liquid in his duffel bag, and as soon as the plane reached thirty thousand feet and the seat-belt signs were turned off—Kaboom! I would either unleash a liquid bomb or just get everyone wet. But really, really wet. So wet they would be terrorized with wetness.

Rather than feel animosity toward my fellow travelers, I sympathized with them. After all, they thought I was trying to kill them, and even though I wasn't, it was probably terrifying to have to walk around an airport knowing someone like me was nearby. I fit the profile—Middle Eastern male, between eighteen and thirty-five, Muslim, sometimes smarmy looking. The fact is, I was thirty at the time, so if I were a terrorist I would probably be at the tail end of my career. Terrorists are like football players in that they have short careers—the better the terrorist, the shorter the career.

I'm Iranian but deeply Americanized, as I've been in the United States for most of my life. I love hamburgers, hot dogs, and Budweiser. (That last thing I don't really love, but when I was in my fraternity in college it was the only thing we could afford. Yes, I was in a frat—Zeta Psi—during my "really trying super hard to blend in as an American" days.) I'm not very religious, but I've got Muslim friends whom I respect—does that make me Muslim-ish and, by association, fit me into the profile? The point is, I understood that I could be mistaken for a bad guy, and I felt sorry for the poor people who had to endure my terrifying presence on their flight.

I did not begrudge anyone racially profiling me as I anxiously gripped my boarding pass and headed toward the gate. In fact, I started profiling myself. To begin with, why was I so paranoid if I wasn't doing something illegal? How well did I really know myself? I was born in Iran, after all, and while the September 11 hijackers were from Saudi Arabia and Egypt, innocent people cannot split hairs over geographic subtleties when their lives are in danger. I had packed my own duffel bag. I knew I had not packed a gun or a bomb. I did not own a gun or a bomb—but still I found myself creeping closer to security, wondering if the TSA guards would find the gun or the bomb that I had not packed and did not own.

I knew how it would all play out—me, duffel bag in hand, California driver's license in my front pocket ready to be flashed as proof of my American-ness, everyone else wondering when I was going to unleash my falafel-fueled fury. I would walk slowly through the metal detector and, of course, it would beep.

"What have I done? Someone stop me!"

"It's okay, sir," the security guard would caution. "Probably just your belt buckle."

"That's what they all say. Check my bags. CHECK MY BAGS!"

"The buckle's made of metal, sir. Calm down. It's typically the buckle."

"But you can't be sure. People sneak guns and bombs on planes all the time! These metal detectors aren't perfect! Frisk me, damn it! Anal cavity probe—pronto!"

"You can walk through again if you'd like."

"Someone stop me! It should not be this easy to board an airplane!"

Fortunately, it never came to this because the TSA just let me go through with no hassle. I think the reason was—and if you're al-Qaeda reading this, please skip this section because I don't want you figuring out how to get past the TSA—that I made a point to overenunciate my English. This ensured that they knew I was one of them and not some low-life terrorist. I found myself talking slowly: "Hell-oh my fell-oh American! I am just here to board the air-o-plane! Carry-ons? Just this American flag. That is ALL I am carrying on!"

And so, it was settled, I was not a terrorist. Or was I?

Maybe I *Am* a Terrorist

Doubts about my own innocence were innate by early 2009, when I landed in Denver to do some shows at the Denver Improv.

I had not been following the news that day. A white guy from the club picked me up and immediately asked me what I thought about the arrest of Zazi, the terror suspect. I had no idea what he was talking about. He figured since I was of Middle Eastern descent, I would have an inside track. (I get these types of questions often: "What do you think of the recent hike in gas prices?" "Why are your people so pissed off?" "When is the next terrorist hit going down?")

I learned that the man's full name was Najibullah Zazi and that he had been a Denver cab driver accused of planning suicide bombings in New York City subways. I didn't think much of the case, but it was a bit suspicious that this guy had been arrested the same day I arrived in Denver.

A few months later I was in Austin, Texas, doing a show and I had to drive to Houston in the morning. When I woke up, I turned on CNN to find a report about a guy flying his plane into the IRS building in Austin. I couldn't believe it. What were the chances that I would be in Austin the same day there was a terrorist attack in that city? I watched and prayed that it wouldn't be a Middle Easterner, and to my relief it turned out to be a disgruntled white guy. But then again, I'm Iranian. Iranians are white. Hmmm . . . Once again, I was beginning to suspect I was up to no good.

Soon after I was at Los Angeles International Airport flying to Philadelphia to perform when I saw a headline in the newspaper about a lady named Jihad Jane. She had been arrested for trying to recruit al-Qaeda operatives out of her home in, where else, Philadelphia. Again, she was a white lady, but she had turned to a life of terrorism and acquired a cute Arab-sounding nickname. That I had been near these activities three times now was beginning to concern me. The fact that two of the wrongdoers were white people gave me a bit of relief. I was keeping score: White people: 2, Middle Easterners: 1.

It didn't end there. A few months later, I was performing at Carolines on Broadway in New York City. One night the cab I was taking to the club had trouble getting me there because of heavy traffic, so I got out and walked. We did our first show and afterward one of the opening acts tried to leave the area. He came back telling us that Times Square had been shut down because of terrorist activity. We turned on the TV to see reports of a Pakistani male who had parked a car in Times Square in an attempt to blow it up. This was the fourth time I was in the vicinity where terrorist activity took place. Maybe I really *was* a terrorist, somehow tied to all of these activities and brainwashed as a child like Angelina Jolie in the movie *Salt* (sorry if I just ruined *Salt* for you)—just waiting to hear the secret word and launch into my mission.

The Joke-Telling Terrorist

It occurred to me that being a comedian really was the perfect cover for a terrorist. Comedians tell jokes. We make observations. We encourage people to smile. No one would ever suspect me of plotting a jihad.

I can imagine the terrorist pep talk:

"Go to America, become a stand-up comedian, spend years touring the country and honing your material. Then, when I give the order, KILL THEM ALL!"

"By 'kill them all,' do you mean kill them with laughter?"

"No, I mean kill them with bullets."

"But what if I'm having a great set? Can I at least wait until the set is over before I kill?"

"No. You must kill when I say kill."

"Do you know how hard it is to kill? Not kill as in kill, but kill as in have a great set."

"You've become very confusing since you chose stand-up as your cover. I told you it would have been easier if you had gone undercover as a chiropractor."

What's funny about all of these events is that I noticed anytime a white person terrorized America, no organization came out to tie itself to that person. However, anytime a Middle Easterner or Muslim committed some sort of terrorist act, an organization would take credit for it and then all Muslims and Middle Easterners would be profiled. When the white guy flew his plane into the IRS building, most people came out and said, "Well, that guy's a nut." Even the Tea Party was adamant: "He's not with us. Probably doesn't even drink tea. But you know who does drink tea? A-rabs! And they're not with us either. So that must mean that the guy who flew his plane into the IRS building was a secret A-rab!" Even though he was white.

However, when the Pakistani guy tried to detonate the car bomb in Times Square, the Pakistani Taliban took credit for the failed bombing. Why would you take credit for a failed car bombing? Why would you call a press conference and say, "We just want to say . . . we tried. And furthermore, it is the thought that counts. And in conclusion, win some, lose some."

The Buddhist Terrorist

This is a theme of my life that continues even today. In the spring of 2012, I did a show in Monaco; a week later a Muslim man went on a shooting spree killing Jews in Toulouse, just a few hours from where I had performed. A year later, I did a show in Colorado Springs; a month after that a white supremacist killed a pizza delivery guy and a Colorado prison chief. These were tragedies, of course, but I found that I could incorporate them into my stand-up by poking fun at my proximity to each event, and audiences would laugh along with me.

Then a big one hit a little too close to home. I was in Boston for a show on April 5, 2013. Just ten days later, the Boston Marathon bombings occurred blocks from where I had performed. Like most Americans, I watched the images and followed the aftermath on TV and Twitter. My thoughts were with the victims and their families. It occurred to me how crazy the world was, how easily people are influenced. What if a young, Middle Eastern Lex Luthor had caught my act in Boston about how I kept showing up around these horrible calamities and thought: *Well, Maz Jobrani was here ten days ago. No better time than now to kill a bunch of innocent people gathered for a life-affirming event such as a marathon.* I honestly had that thought for a second. That's how deep this feeling of guilt had gone, stupid though it may sound. But weirder shit has happened. Remember John Hinckley Jr., who shot President Reagan in 1981? He was trying to impress actress Jodie Foster and was inspired by the movie *Taxi Driver.* You never know what inspires a crazy mind. What if my stupid jokes were inspiring this madness?

As I watched the stories of the Boston bombing unfold, I realized how paranoid I had become. I just hoped whoever had done it, they didn't turn out to be Middle Eastern. When it was revealed that the bombers were from Chechnya, I was relieved, wandering the room with arms raised in victory: "Hell yeah, it wasn't us this time!" Chechnya is in the Caucasus region of Russia, which meant these guys were literally Caucasian. Score! Then it came out they were Muslim: "Dammit! Why can't it be another religion for once? Why couldn't they be Buddhists?" (On a side note, Buddhists make lousy terrorists because they live in the moment. A Buddhist terrorist would think, *I was going to blow myself up . . . but that moment is gone. I'm in another moment now. I don't feel very explosive. I feel like dancing.*)

Days after the Boston Marathon bombings, a fertilizer plant blew up in West, Texas—right near Dallas, where I had performed the weekend before. Could there be a group of comedy enthusiasts—who either loved or despised my act—following me around the country, performing terrorist acts, and waiting for the FBI to make the connection? Then it hit me: I travel too much, and the world is batshit crazy. Perhaps crazier than it's ever been.

There have always been lunatics, but it feels in the time of the Internet and jumbo jets and reality television that things have become even more absurd. In this day of instant media we hear about attacks faster, and it seems like we're becoming more violent as a result. You would think that we would have evolved and come to the realization that killing innocent people and fighting religious wars is ignorant. You can't blame a whole people because someone from one background does something stupid and violent. If a white guy kills a black guy it doesn't mean that all white people hate all black people. If a Muslim kills a Jew it doesn't mean that all Muslims hate all Jews. It's time we all came together and realized that it's the North Koreans we need to hate. They're the ones to blame for EVERYTHING!

When the Boston bombers were revealed to be Chechen, some people posted on Twitter that we should bomb the Czech Republic. This was further proof of how stupid and crazy people have become in this age of technological advances. First of all, if you are Tweeting that means that you are on your phone or computer and you could move your mouse six little inches to Google and find out that Chechens aren't from the Czech Republic. They're from Chechnya. Six inches, that's the difference between a smart racist and a stupid racist. Second, you don't bomb an entire country because of the actions of two people. (I know we have in the past, but that was nineteen people and we bombed the wrong country.)

I grew so tired of reading stupid stuff from stupid people online that I came up with an app to cure this epidemic. I am calling it the Twitslap app. It's an app where you can slap somebody for saying something stupid online. I want to have a hand come out of the mobile device where someone is writing something stupid and actually slap him. I haven't perfected the technology, but if an engineer is reading this and knows how to do it, please get in touch with me @MazJobrani. If all goes well we can move to Facebook next to create Faceslap. Then YouTube for Youslap. Then Yahoo for Yahooslap. Okay, fine, that one needs a little work.

Casey Kasem Was Arab

In 2008, I had traveled to Denver to perform, and there was no terrorist activity. Instead there was hope. It was the Democratic National Convention and the Arab American Institute had organized a comedy show with Middle Eastern comedians. This was after eight years of George W. Bush, and we were all sick of being portrayed as bad guys and enemies of America. Barack Obama gave us hope that we could come out of 2008 with a positive change to our image and a more level playing field.

A limousine picked us up from the airport. I assumed we would be driven in a Toyota Prius, which has much lower emissions than a limo, given that the Democrats were going to change everything that was wrong under Bush. But the limo company was owned by an Arab, so it probably was given to the Arab American Institute for a discount. For some reason Arabs and Persians own a lot of limousine companies. I'm guessing it's so they can make money driving people around and then when they need a car for a fancy party they can just pick one out of the garage and look good pulling up to the valet.

We took our limo ride to the venue and were received with open arms by all the politically active Middle Easterners, Muslims, and liberal white people who had come to see us. We felt like we were part of a big wave of change. We even had a U.S. congressman stop by our show to give a speech of support. It was such a great night that the other comedians and I decided to celebrate between shows with a few drinks.

By the time the second show began, I was feeling loose onstage. I even felt like riffing a bit on my prepared material and had a wonderful time. All was well until a week later. I got an e-mail from a man saying he had been at the second show and was ashamed of me for being on drugs. I had no idea what he was talking about as I don't do drugs, so I e-mailed him back to make sure he was talking about me. He told me that he was an Iranian American who had been in law enforcement and he was adept at telling when people are drugged out. He felt that as a role model in the community, I needed to set a better example.

At this point, most people would tell this guy to go fuck himself. But I'm a peaceful and diplomatic person so I explained to this gentleman that while I'd had a few drinks, I did not use drugs. After a little back and forth he came around and we actually became friends . . . or acquaintances. Okay, we became people who text each other once in a while, although really not that much, and typically as a mistake. Fine—he's a contact in my phone and I don't know how to delete him.

But through this experience, I realized something. Even scarier and more laden with responsibility than being mistaken for a terrorist—how had I become mistaken for a role model? It occurred to me that our community had not had many people that it could cling to as role models in this country. We've had so much bad press and such a horrible image in the mainstream media that when someone like me shows up, no matter how small my success, the community embraces him as a role model. Whereas Italians had Al Pacino and Joe DiMaggio, Jews had Steven Spielberg and Sandy Koufax, African Americans had Sidney Poitier and Michael Jordan, Middle Easterners had Casey Kasem and the Iron Sheik. I bet you didn't know Casey Kasem was Arab. Ask any Arab and they will tell you, "Oh yes, he was one of us." Middle Easterners will talk your ear off about how many people in America are undercover Middle Easterners, meaning they don't really talk about their Middle Eastern-ness in the media. Casey Kasem, Salma Hayek, Tony Shalhoub, Danny Thomas, Freddie Mercury, Paul Anka, Shannon Elizabeth, Vince Vaughn, Jerry Seinfeld (whose mother was born in Syria), Andre Agassi, Tom Cruise . . . okay that last one is made up, but you never know, his real name might be Taymour Khoroos. "Khoroos" means "rooster" in Persian, so that could be why he changed his name. I'm just saying.

Back to my point. Maybe I don't want to be a role model. How are role models chosen? One doesn't apply to be a role model. Role models are simply appointed, which isn't really fair. What if you want to pick your nose and drink beer in public? What if you want to pick your nose WHILE drinking beer in public? Can you pick your nose and drink beer at the same time? What if you have fat fingers and can't get them up your nose while you're drinking in public? If you're a role model, you have to think through all these minute-to-minute decisions.

I have since come to embrace the position, albeit reluctantly. The problem with accepting that you're a role model is that it allows critics within the community to scrutinize your every move. I am a board member of an organization called the Persian American Cancer Institute, which tries to get Iranians to sign up for the bone marrow registry so that when another Iranian needs a bone marrow transplant we have a good resource. One of our projects was to inspire younger people to sign up using a funny video. I proposed we do a video where there is a guy procrastinating and not signing up. Part of this guys' character is that he farts a lot. The reason I chose to have him fart was because I figured that would help young people enjoy the video and get the message to them in a lighthearted way. Look, I'm a comedian—even when the topic is bone cancer, farts make me laugh.

When we posted the video, I got e-mails from people in the Iranian community condemning my use of lowbrow humor. "How dare you put out such a video? You are a role model. I expected more from you." And that is why I can never *fully* embrace the role model position. I believe that in life you need to stay true to your principles. If you begin to give in to what others expect of you, then you're done, especially as an artist. So let me be clear right now. I am standing by my principles: Farts are funny.

Don't Wear a Backpack at Home Depot

When you're a comedian you travel the world doing your gig for people from America to Canada to Europe to the Middle East.

Some people see my schedule and say, "Man, you are so lucky. You've seen the world." A lot of the time I fly in the night before, do my set, and leave the next day. Most spare time is spent trying to catch up on sleep. So whereas people think I've seen the world, I've actually seen a lot of nice hotel rooms around the world. With some of the cities I travel to, the clubs are located in the suburbs. So there have been times when I forget which city I'm in. One time when I was in Denver, I looked out my hotel window to see a Home Depot across the freeway. I had to think for a minute whether I was in Denver or Dallas. And if I was looking for a little mindless entertainment to pass the time, the Home Depot constituted all of the options within walking distance.

There's actually a lot to do inside a Home Depot. The stores are like small countries. You can browse the power tools. You can check out all the innovations they've made in kitchen fixtures. You can buy the light bulbs your wife has been asking you to buy for months, although you haven't had the time to actually go to a Home Depot in your hometown. But if there's one thing I've learned as a Middle Eastern American, it's that when you go to Home Depot looking like me, you should not go wearing a backpack. Backpacks on a Middle Easterner or a Muslim in any place—other than a university or a backpack store—are cause for concern. If you don't believe me, ask the two Moroccan guys who were the original suspects in the Boston Marathon bombings. They had their pictures plastered on the front cover of the *New York Post*—and only because they were brown guys wearing backpacks at the site of the bombings. It was later proven that they were innocent, but I guarantee you they learned this lesson: Next time at a public event, fanny packs only.

New York, New York

New York holds a special place in my heart. It was the first city I arrived in when I came to America in late 1978. Whenever I see movies from that era I feel nostalgic for the Big Apple—films like *Saturday Night Fever*, with John Travolta as Tony Manero. Yes, I get emotional when I see John Travolta dance. Don't judge me. This just means I'm in touch with my feminine side. Must be all the soymilk I've been drinking lately. Did you know soymilk increases your estrogen levels? I didn't either until I woke up one morning with breasts—really cute, perky ones, I finally decided, after staring at them in the mirror for a solid three hours. I should've known something was wrong when I began watching *Sex and the City* reruns with my wife and her friends, sipping rosé wine and relaxing in my yoga pants.

But I digress. I didn't actually see *Saturday Night Fever* in 1978.

Back then I had no idea who John Travolta was. My first exposure to his films came a couple years later when we moved to Marin County. The family friends we first stayed with had a heavyset son named Mohammad who loved the movie *Grease*. He and his female cousin, Mahnaz, would reenact the film's final dance scene for me and my sister, who were a few years younger and new to America. I was in awe of how cool these two were when they would turn on Mohammad's record player to the final song—"You're the One That I Want"—flick on a strobe light, and perform the full dance for us. My favorite moment of our private *Grease* show was when Mohammad would drop to his knees like Travolta does at seeing Olivia Newton-John in her digs and looking sexy. The only difference being that Travolta was a lean Italian dude in a cool black outfit and greased-back hair while Mohammad was a plump Iranian ten-year-old in ill-fitting clothes and prescription glasses that would roll down the tip of his nose every time he did the drop. Not to mention that given Mohammad's weight, the whole floor of the house shook whenever he landed on his knees. The first time this happened, I thought we were experiencing one of the famous Californian earthquakes. Even back then I knew my friends' attempt at being cool Americans wasn't really working, but I never let on. After all, I was fresh off the boat. Who was I to judge?

Anyway, *Saturday Night Fever* makes me emotional for the New York City portion of my childhood—FAO Schwarz, fancy hotels, room service that brought strawberries and whipped cream every night. Maybe that's why I miss those days—when I was six, I could eat all the whipped cream I wanted. Now, if I add whipped cream to any food I will spend two days beating myself up for eating unhealthy. I have a weird, middle age, suburban eating disorder. I tend to go through my days eating pretty well—tuna sandwiches,

"I mean no insult to your ancestors. However, I insist, I pay!"

"If you pay, I will never talk to you again!"

"If you pay, I will be forced to report you and your family to immigration and have you deported so that you will never be able to pay in America again!"

"If you pay, I will have you executed so you will never be able to pay on earth again!"

"That settles it. I will see you in hell! How much tip do I leave on twenty-seven fifty-two?"

My father was constantly going through these battles whenever we were dining with other Persians. When we ate with American friends, it was my dad saying, "I pay!" And the Americans responding, "Okay, sure, that works."

It was not that our American friends were cheap. It's just a cultural thing with us Persians. I would watch as my dad would pay all the bills and it made me feel proud. I would celebrate most of these meals with my strawberry and whipped cream desserts and I would feel on top of the world. It was great being a six-year-old on a sugar high with a dad who paid for everything.

When we were driving home from one of these New York dinners one night, my dad drank so much that he put his foot out the passenger side window and began to dance. He turned up the music and wiggled his leg at oncoming traffic. He didn't seem to care if anyone noticed. He wasn't even worried that the cops would see him and think he was acting belligerent. To me, a young boy, he looked like he was a king, enjoying life without worrying about repercussions. It was only later that I came to understand my father was a functioning alcoholic. Orange juice and vodka was to him what Starbucks macchiatos are to people today. "I will take a venti vodka orange juice please, no foam. And add a shot." I was too young to know the difference, clapping along in the backseat and enjoying the show.

This wasn't the first time I had been in a car with my dad when he'd been drinking. In Tehran years earlier, we were on our way home from a party and came across a pack of wild dogs roaming our neighborhood. For no reason I can recall, my dad, who was driving this time, pulled the car over and got out, wearing a nice suit and dress shoes. He had been hitting the drink that night, so he was in king mode. He grabbed a rock and started chasing the dogs while yelling at them. He didn't consider that these were wild dogs that might rip him apart for a meal. When you're in king mode you can take on anything—even wild animals foaming at the mouth. I, of course, adored it—my brave father taking on a pack of dogs, in dress shoes no less!

In hindsight, it was the vodka that made him so brave. He hadn't thought through what he planned on doing if the dogs attacked him. When you're that drunk you probably don't spend a lot of time thinking about what comes next after they don't run away. Either way, he managed to scare them off and survived that episode. Considering this story years later, it occurs to me there are several things wrong with it.

First—and to point out the obvious—he was driving drunk. But in the early 1970s in Tehran that was not a big deal. I believe the rule then was that as long as you're conscious, then you're okay to drive. If the cops pulled you over they would administer the field sobriety test, which in Iran was basically the ability to stand on your own two feet and dance like you're turning a light bulb. That's the national Iranian dance. Try it. It's a lot of fun. Just hold your hands in the air and act like you're screwing in a light bulb. Now turn your hips as you do that and, voilà, you're proficient at both dancing Persian and passing an Iranian field sobriety test. If you got out of the car and fell flat on your face, then that was it. They would take your keys from you. Of course, if you could touch your nose with your fingers while you were flat on your back then they would reconsider and give you a second chance at the test. If you could screw the light bulb while you were on the ground, they would turn up the radio and actually buy you a drink.

Second, my dad was driving drunk with his young son and daughter in the backseat NOT buckled into seat belts. Again, in the mid-1970s in Tehran that was par for the course. Why would you put a seat belt on your kids? That would just make it harder to get them out if there was an accident. If you left them loose in the backseat then in case of an accident they would just fly out of the car and land on the sidewalk, or a cushiony crowd of bystanders. Also, back then and even today we didn't have child seats in the Middle East. To us a child seat was grandma's lap.

Last, reflecting on Dad versus Wild Dogs, I realize there's an issue PETA members might have with him chasing the dogs with a rock. For any animal activist planning a case against my father, let me assure you that the dogs were wild and possibly dangerous. Furthermore, I don't think my dad actually threw the rock at them, but I can't be sure of that. I was too busy wrestling with my sister in the back of the car to get a good look. In Iran, for the most part, dogs aren't accepted as pets as they are in America. Pets are roosters and hens, and sometimes they get names, and sometimes they get eaten. This is bad news, of course, for the kids who grow attached to Rahim the rooster but good news for the parents who use Rahim to impregnate all the other hens, then eat the horny bird. Also, Iranians keep their parents and grandparents in their homes until they die, so we're too busy cleaning up after our relatives to chase dogs. While in America people chase their parents out of the house, in Iran we chase dogs out of the house. Either way, someone has to go.

Later in life, as my dad got older and lost most of his money in bad investments, he told me he had wanted to buy a building in Midtown Manhattan when we first came to America.

"Today dat building is vorth von hundred fifty million dollars. I could have been king of New York, dancing vith my feet out the vindow every night on Fifth Avenue. But your mom vanted to go to California for sunshine. I never should have listened to her. Dat sun cost me a hundred and fifty million dollars."

When I told my mom this, she had a different take: "You know how cold deh vinters are in New York? He put his foot out deh vindow so much he vould have died from ferostbite. And you vere too eh-skinny to survive dat veather. That's vhy ve fed you so much eh-strawberries and vhipped keeream. Ve vere terying to make you pelump for the vinters. Anyvay, your father vould have lost dat money, too. It is a good ting I talked him out of it. At least he got a tan!"

What Would Sofia Vergara Do?

In 2006, I lived in New York during the taping of a short-lived TV show I did for ABC called *The Knights of Prosperity*. This was a show about a group of low-income workers who were down and out on their luck. In order to make some money, they decided to rob Mick Jagger. It starred Donal Logue as a janitor who had come up with the idea and it had a cast of six people. I played Gourishankar Subramaniam, the Indian cab driver who was also a womanizer and served as the driver of the group's getaway car. The female member of the group was a diner waitress played by Sofia Vergara. It was a very funny show, top-notch writing, great critical reviews, and subsequently canceled by the eighth or ninth episode.

People don't realize how tough it is to get on a hit sitcom. I've had people come up to me and say, "Maz, you should be on that show! You'd be great. You should call the producers and have them put you on it." I wish it were that easy.

"Hello? Is this the production office of *Louie*? Yes, I would like to submit myself to play the part of Louie. Oh, Louie is playing Louie? How about his brother? Cousin? Neighbor? Those parts don't exist? Hmmm. Can I at least serve coffee at production meetings? Great, see you in the morning!"

Here's how it really works. Each year, from around the end of summer until early fall, the major networks ABC, CBS, NBC, and FOX hear pitches for shows. I don't know what the exact number is, but I know it's a lot of pitches, probably in the hundreds. From those pitches they will order a bunch of scripts. From those scripts they will then order pilot episodes for a handful of shows. I think the year I did *Knights of Prosperity*, ABC ordered ten or twelve comedy pilots. A pilot is just one episode of the show that the networks will spend millions to make and then focus-group. From the pilots shot, they will then choose about four or five of those shows to put on the air in the fall. In 2006, *The Knights of Prosperity* had been chosen as one of the shows for ABC. I auditioned and got the part.

The auditioning process is ruthless. You're up against hundreds of people gunning for one part. The closer you get, the more the pressure builds. This culminates in something called a network test, where they will narrow the part down to three or four actors and have you all come in at the same time and audition in front of the show's producers as well as the heads of the network and the studio. It's especially nerve-wracking because before you go in for the final audition, they've already negotiated your contract, so you know that if you get the part you stand to make tens of thousands of dollars a week. Of course, should you end up blowing it, you're back to making lattes at Starbucks.

I remember other comedians congratulating me for getting the part. "Congrats man! You made it!" I would remind them that TV is very competitive and just because I was on a pilot that didn't mean that I had made it. I didn't really know how competitive it was until our show finally aired. The network premiered it in January 2007. The first night our show came on was during the college football bowl season; we were on at the same time as the Sugar Bowl, which took away a lot of our potential viewers. The second week, President Bush gave a speech just as our show began. That bumped us from our time slot and took away any momentum we might have built from the previous week. (Thanks again, George W., my constant nemesis. First you put Iran into your axis of evil, then you give a speech during my sitcom.) The third week we were on, FOX premiered *American Idol*, which at the time was attracting tens of millions of viewers each week. They killed us in the ratings. It occurred to me that if I had just learned to be a mediocre singer, it would have improved my career in television.

As I watched us sink week by week, I grew more nervous. What was going to be next? I imagined seeing an ad on FOX: "Next week, the TV event of a lifetime. Jesus comes back. One night only!" Great! Now we had to compete with Armageddon? Jesus never came back, but neither did our show. We were canceled shortly after and I went back to auditioning. One step further from a hit show and one step closer to serving lattes at Starbucks.

Back then, Sofia Vergara had not been on *Modern Family,* so she was not as well known as she is now. My experience with her and the whole cast was really great. Besides being beautiful, she was incredibly cool and fun to work with. Being a regular on the show, I had my mother come to visit one time from Los Angeles. She was impressed with the show and thought Sofia was charming and beautiful. Years later, after *The Knights of Prosperity* had been canceled and *Modern Family* became the biggest hit on TV, I got a call from my mother.

"You need to change agents."

"What are you talking about?"

"Your career. It eh-stinks I'm eh-smelling it from vay over here in Vestwood."

"Mom, why are you being so dramatic? I live fifteen minutes away from you. Besides, I'm doing fine."

"Just fine? Sofia isn't doing just fine. She do amazing. I saw her on cover of *Elle* magazine. You should be on cover of *Elle* magazine."

"*Elle* is a woman's magazine."

"So vhat? You need to tink outside the package. I bet Sofia's agents tink outside the package."

"You mean outside the box."

"Box, package . . . same ting. You should be on *Modern Family.* You are modern. You have a family. Call and tell dem to put you on."

"It doesn't work that way. You have to audition against hundreds of people, land the pilot, get picked up, and hope people watch it. It's really competitive."

"How about *American Idol?* You are kind of a mediocre singer. Have you thought about getting on dat?"

"No, Mom. I don't want to be a singer."

"How about a lawyer?"

"What?"

"Plumber? *American Plumber* sounds nice."

"Mom! Stop giving me career advice."

"You have to ask yourself, 'Vhat vould Sofia do?'"

"So she's Jesus now?"

"Yes, but vith better hair. And a hit show."

Nearly Killed by a Cod

I almost died in New York while filming *The Knights of Prosperity*. Not from a mugging or nearly getting hit by a cab, but by a fish. In 2006 when I was working on the show, I had a horrible experience one day with a cod. When you are on a film or TV show they provide lunch for you. That day the fish was cod. Later that night as I was being dropped off at my apartment, I began to feel a bit nauseous. I rushed to the bathroom to relieve myself, only to discover the impossible duality of also having to vomit. There is no worse feeling than having food poisoning and the poison insisting on leaving your body through multiple orifices. It's a life-altering moment when you have to decide which end of your body gets to use the toilet first.

As I was caught in this anatomical conundrum, underwear at my knees, I had the added sensation of suffocation. I didn't know it at the time, but I was hyperventilating. Apparently, my lungs didn't want to miss out on all the fun my intestines were having. If you've never hyperventilated, I highly recommend doing it in a crowded space, never alone in your bathroom. First, you get light-headed. Then just as you're about to black out, you think, *Oh hell no!*

No way I'm blacking out from breathing too heavy. Especially with my underwear at my knees. This is NOT gonna happ . . . And boom, you're out.

Next thing I knew, I awoke in my own crime scene—facedown on the bathroom floor, underwear now at my ankles, blood on the wall. I had hit the towel holder with the back of my head as I fell and it cut a gash. Luckily I had not hit it hard enough to cause serious bleeding. This was a major relief because the last way you want to die would be from eating the wrong fish. I can imagine my funeral.

"Maz died in a fish accident."

"He was attacked by a shark?"

"No, it was a cod."

"A cod ate him?"

"No, he ate the cod."

"So then how did he die?"

"I just told you. The cod killed him."

"A cop killed Maz?"

"NO! COD! C-O-D!"

"Cash on delivery? It was a drug deal? I knew it. He was always up to something fishy."

"No! It was a fish. Food poisoning. He died hyperventilating with his underwear at his ankles."

"Whoa. He was eating fish with his pants off? That's some kinky shit."

My near-death-by-cod experience during *The Knights of Prosperity* filming may have been a sign from the heavens of how the show was going to do. But such cosmic signals did not land until years later. While driving in Los Angeles, I saw a homeless person wearing an orange T-shirt that we wore in the show with the words "The Knights of Prosperity." Seeing a homeless woman with a

T-shirt from the show that I had been on just a couple of years earlier reminded me just how fast life can go from promising to unfortunate. Maybe my mom was right. Maybe I did need new agents. "Vhat vould Sofia do?" I asked myself. I was never going to have her hair. Instead, I took mom's advice and fired my agents.

September 11

The morning of September 11, 2001, I was in Los Angeles. Like many people, I could not believe what I was watching on TV. It was heartbreaking to see all the misery and even more heartbreaking because it was happening to New York, which will always hold a special place in my heart. At the time, my younger brother, Kashi, was working near the Twin Towers, so my first instinct was to call and make sure he was okay. Once that had been confirmed I drove around Los Angeles visiting my family, in shock.

As the day went on, I seriously considered never performing comedy again. Not because I was of Middle Eastern descent, but because of the sadness that consumed me. How could anything ever be funny again? Life just seemed very tragic. Just a few days later I was scheduled to do a show at a private residence in Irvine, California. I thought for sure the show would be canceled, but when I called to check in, the host pleaded with me to perform. He told me that his wife was Turkish and that the guests were all very open-minded. He suggested that laughter was needed, now more than ever.

Hesitantly, I confirmed my appearance. America had become so crazy in those days that I honestly feared for my life. What if one of the guests decided to attack me because I was Iranian? Was this some sort of setup? Was the guy's wife really Turkish? Did

Turkey even qualify as a Middle Eastern country? I thought they were trying to join the European Union. That would mean they're European. Everyone knows Europeans hate Iranians. So by default the Turks must hate Iranians. This had to be a setup!

I went onstage—on their patio, actually, as the event was outdoors—and began my set. I don't think I had ever taken so long during a performance to reveal my ethnicity. It was a thirty-minute set. I did the first ten minutes without mentioning my background. I'm sure the guests were suspicious: "Where is this guy from? He looks Middle Eastern, but maybe he's Mexican. Let's give him a few minutes before we lynch him."

Finally when I got up the nerve to mention ethnicity, I professed it with some regret. "I am an American citizen and have grown up in America," I began. "I have to tell you, it's been a crazy week. So crazy that I find myself being a fan of George W. Bush. I am fully on board with him and hope we catch these terrorists! Anyway, even though I am American, I was born in Iran." Being outdoors, you could actually hear the crickets. "I know, I know, I'm not a fan of that either. Before I go any further please join me in singing the Turkish national anthem in honor of our hostess this evening. Also, anyone who is interested can follow me to the maid's quarters where I will allow you to waterboard me to show my allegiance to this great country of ours. USA! USA!"

I didn't actually go that far, but looking out at the guests it sure felt like they were contemplating torturing me, or at the very least calling the FBI. Those were tense times, and just saying you were Middle Eastern was cause for concern. I kept waiting for the Turkish hostess to come up and give me a hug, but she never did. She was probably afraid the guests were there to get her, too. Where the hell was she? Maybe she was hiding in the closet. Either way, the show had to go on, and my set basically turned into a speech about my allegiance to the United States. If I knew how to play the guitar, I would have started singing Kid Rock songs.

As the weeks went on, I realized there was an important role comedy would play in healing the tragedies of September 11. Comedy can help people cope, and many fans were coming to the clubs to laugh out the stress. My fellow comedians agreed that the crowds were laughing louder than ever after September 11. It was as if they were in therapy at the clubs. Another role that comedy would serve was to bring a voice of reason to an irrational time. It was not too long after the attacks when I began to notice how patriotism was blinding people to basic morality. Individuals were going around shooting anyone wearing a turban. This, unfortunately, caused many Indian Sikhs to be targeted. On a national level, I saw that the Bush administration was using the attacks as an excuse to start a war with Iraq and Afghanistan. More than ever, it was my job to talk about these issues onstage and try to bring them to light in a funny, accessible way.

Easier said than done.

One of our first shows as the Arabian Knights after September 11 was in La Jolla, California. We had not put that name on our show for about six months. When we dared to call it that again—we put it up on the marquee in a town very close to Marine Corps Base Camp Pendleton—we actually received a death threat. Someone called the club and said he would be coming to take us out. The club manager brought this to the attention of me, Ahmed Ahmed and Aron Kader (the other Arabian Knights) and asked if we wanted to cancel the show. We all agreed that it was an empty threat and that we would go on with the performance. Fortunately, no one bombed that night, on or off the stage.

A giant pet peeve of mine after September 11 was when morning radio deejays would interview us Axis of Evil comedians and make assumptions: "So September eleventh really helped your careers, no?" This was insulting, ignorant, and racist. I would remind them that as an Iranian I had been dealing with being demonized since the hostage crisis. It wasn't as if I started doing stand-up right after September 11. I had been doing comedy before and I had spoken about many other topics beyond my ethnicity. These deejays were free to say such things to us because attacking Middle Easterners, Muslims, and Arabs was accepted. I doubt they would have asked a black comedian if slavery was what helped his career.

Our perseverance paid off, and one of the highlights of our tour came in New York years later. In the fall of 2007, the Axis of Evil tour arrived to do two sold-out shows at the Nokia Theater on Broadway. This was the coolest thing up to that point in my career. Our names were in bright lights on Broadway. I went down to the theater and took hundreds of pictures as the marquee lit up: "Maz Jobrani." I didn't care how dorky I looked. I'm pretty sure Bono doesn't stand outside the venues where he performs to snap pictures of his name, but I didn't care. This was huge. We had made it to Broadway. My bigger concern was that a cop would see me and think I was casing the joint as a target for al-Qaeda.

All those years after arriving in America I found my name in lights in the greatest city on earth. As Frank Sinatra said, "If I can make it there, I'll make it anywhere." In celebration, that night my wife and I went back to our hotel room and conceived our first child. I'm not sure if Frank's words encompassed making babies, but that night in New York they did.

Now you may be asking how I know that was the night when we made our first boy, Dhara. It wasn't that we were making love every nine months and then waiting to see what happened. (Though that would be one way to do it.) No, we know that was the night because we both left town afterward for business trips. She went to Italy and I to the Middle East. I know where your head is at: "Italy, huh? How do you know he's not the love child of some guy named Giuseppe?" I'm going to defer to my keen eye and say that the kid has my mouth. I've observed it in many ways, doing my own little version of a DNA test, and I have concluded that the tongue, lips, and mouth belong to me. So until I run into a guy named Giuseppe who's got those same lips, mouth, and tongue, I know my theory is in good standing. *Grazie!*

While my wife left the Big Apple to go to Italy on business I was heading to the Middle East with the Axis of Evil Comedy Tour. It was the first time that a group of American comedians would be performing for the people of the region. I would be re-inventing myself from a failed sitcom actor to a purveyor of world peace. Years before, I had left the Middle East to come to New York, and now I was leaving New York to head to the Middle East. To borrow another Jesus analogy, it felt a little like the messiah was coming home. Although in this reference, the messiah couldn't walk on water or turn water into wine. He was arriving in business class hoping his jokes would go over without getting heckled. Jesus died for their sins. I was dying for their approval.

Part Three

The Persian Elvis (a.k.a. Pelvis)

Dubai, UAE

Toward the end of 2007 I traveled to Dubai with the Axis of Evil Comedy Tour. Our special had come out on Comedy Central earlier that year, and it was the first time there was a show on American TV with a Middle Eastern cast in which we didn't all get killed. (The comics included me, Ahmed Ahmed and Aron Kader, who were the founding members, as well as Dean Obeidallah, who was brought on as the fourth performer on the special.) This was progress for all Middle Eastern performers in Hollywood because everyone knows that the first step in having a successful career is to not die. Things were looking up, and our live shows were packed with new Middle Eastern fans coming out in droves. As my comedy friend Sam Tripoli said, I was becoming the Persian Elvis, a.k.a. Pelvis.

The special also made a big splash in the Middle Eastern and

Muslim communities around the world. After our clips were seen on YouTube, we gained some fame and were invited to Dubai to kick off a five-country tour of the region. This was a big deal because no American-based comedy troupe had ever gone to the Middle East to perform for Middle Eastern people. As a matter of fact, normally whenever Middle Easterners hear the words "American" and "troop" in the same sentence, it usually means their country is about to be attacked. So it was important for us to emphasize the word "comedy" when publicizing our Dubai arrival. It was also important for us to spell troupe with a "u." What a difference a vowel makes.

When past American comedians have visited foreign countries, it was usually to perform on a military base for U.S. troops. USO tours, featuring some of the biggest names in entertainment, have long flown to parts of the world where the United States is at war. It has always been an honor for a performer to entertain soldiers fighting for our freedoms. But actually going to entertain the people we're historically fighting *against* was less common. What if Bob Hope had done a show for the Vietcong? What if Jessica Simpson had sung for Saddam Hussein's army? Judging by how Tony Romo's career as the Dallas Cowboys quarterback seemed to go south after he dated Simpson, maybe her performing for Saddam would have led to his downfall, too. Who needed Operation Shock and Awe when we could've given them Operation Look Pretty and Lip-Synch? (I know it was Jessica's sister, Ashlee, who famously got caught lip-synching on *Saturday Night Live*, but I'm sure Jessica probably lip-synched at some point in her career. If you don't like what I'm saying about Ms. Simpson, then you can go ahead and Twitslap me.)

We were instantly impressed by Dubai's grandeur. Nothing in

Dubai is small. They have the world's tallest building, one of the world's biggest malls, the greatest fountain—everything is big, big, big. They're so obsessed with setting records that I wouldn't have been surprised if one of the locals had once told me, "Maz, this is the roundest building in the world. Yes, a circle is normally 360 degrees. This building . . . 362 degrees. I swear! We bring engineers from Harvard. I don't know how they do it, but they add two degrees to the circle. It is so round it's almost square!"

And so our first experience in Dubai was also big. I and the other two Axis of Evil comedians, Ahmed Ahmed and Aron Kader, really had no idea what we were in for. Once we got into town we were told by our promoters that there would be a press conference to kick off our tour. Press conference? Who the hell was coming to a press conference for us? What were we, the Blue Collar Comedy Tour? Then we realized—this was Dubai. In Dubai, everything was big, so we were the biggest comedy tour *ever* in the Middle East. We were like the Blue Collar Comedy Tour, but with tans. The Brown Collar Comedy Tour.

I was shocked to discover about fifty journalists and media types all seated and waiting attentively to watch us do a short show followed by a question and answer session. We were just comics trying to be funny. When did we become big-time? Apparently on the flight over the Atlantic. Whatever had changed, we were ready to embrace it. It was interesting performing in the Middle East for the first time because whereas in the United States we were seen as Middle Easterners, the people in the Middle East saw us as Hollywood stars—and ones with a special connection to their people. The reporters at the press conference asked us questions about the difficulties of being Middle Eastern and living in the United States.

"Do you often get profiled at airports when you travel?"

"How do you feel about playing terrorist parts in American movies?"

"Do you think that your Axis of Evil Comedy Tour will help bring peace and understanding to the world?"

"Do they have good baba ghanoush in Los Angeles?"

It began to feel like we were, collectively, the Great Arab Hope (or in my case the Great Persian Hope). Dubai is filled with influential people, and many of them wanted to have meetings with us. "How can we make a movie together?" "How much money will it take to start a studio?" "Can you introduce me to Angelina Jolie?" It was a bit overwhelming.

Meanwhile, our shows in Dubai were selling out faster than any of our shows had in the United States. Everywhere we went, people recognized us. I began to feel like the Eddie Murphy of Dubai. I quickly learned that I *was* the Eddie Murphy of Dubai—only because there was zero chance that Eddie Murphy was ever traveling to Dubai. For better or for worse, we were overnight superstars.

Where Have All the Locals Gone?

One thing you notice in Dubai is that you see local citizens from time to time, but you see many more immigrants. Mainly Indians, Pakistanis, Sri Lankans, and Filipinos. Also, there seems to be a huge disparity in wealth in Dubai. While driving back late from a club after a show, I would look out the window of the luxury car I was being driven in and see a blue bus filled with Pakistani men all barely awake, all in blue outfits, being shuttled home after a hard day of labor in the hot sun. I was told by some locals that these guys leave their home countries with the promise of making money so that they can send it back to their families. Many of them work all day and then go home to sleep in apartments that serve as housing for several men in cramped quarters. They go years without seeing the family they're sending money to and they basically lead miserable lives.

It was something I tried to make sense of as I was living this superstar lifestyle, all of us traveling on the same highway in the middle of the night but going to such different places. It's sad that there isn't more equal distribution of wealth in the world, but that's a bigger problem that someone much smarter than me can explain in a different book than this one.

I tried to do my part by tipping well. It was the least I could do. I always had change on hand so I could tip the bellman, the driver, the housekeeping guy. And they were always very appreciative. I once tipped an Indian guy ten bucks for cleaning my room, and I think I might have paid his mortgage for the month. The rest of my stay, every time I would come out of my room this guy would pop out from behind a different plant and offer to clean my room again.

"Sir, can I clean your room again?"

"Sanjeev, it's already clean."

"Sir, I would like to make it even more clean."

"I'm telling you, Sanjeev, it's very clean."

"Sir, I can make it very, very clean. Please give me this opportunity. Just one opportunity."

I would give in and have to tip him a few more bucks. Spreading the wealth was getting expensive. I was lucky Sanjeev wasn't a meth head. I wouldn't have been able to keep up with his cleaning habit. But I was always amazed at how he was able to actually make it cleaner.

The thing that struck me about Dubai's diversity was that even though it was this place that claimed to have the biggest and the best, it felt like a lot of that was being generated by outsiders. The mystique of the place was imported. One night we were told that we would be taken on an authentic Dubai desert safari at midnight. I was excited as I imagined driving out to the desert to be greeted by Bedouins who had been living out there for hundreds of years. This was going to be the real deal. Maybe I could talk to one of these guys and get a feel for what it's like to live in the desert and hide in the sand to avoid danger. I had stopped taking roles as a terrorist, but maybe a role would come up for a desert Bedouin. I had to be ready. Soon we were en route to the vast and magical desert. I wanted to savor the entire experience so I asked our driver what part of the desert he was from. He told me Turkey.

"You mean there's a region in the desert called Turkey?"

"No, I am from the country of Turkey."

"I see. So you're not a local desert dweller whose family has been living here for generations?"

He looked at me through the rearview mirror and turned up the Michael Jackson playing on his radio.

So what—he wasn't the real deal. I would just wait to find the real deal once we got out into the desert. That was the plan anyway. I soon came to realize that the "authentic" Dubai desert safari was catered by Filipinos who served us Italian food while we watched a Russian belly dancer wiggle her hips in a purple outfit straight out of *I Dream of Jeannie*. Russians are good at drinking vodka, training five-year-olds to compete in the Olympics, and killing you with their bare hands. Belly dancing is not their forte. Don't get me wrong—our Russian Jeannie was good, but she didn't have the extra hip moves that Middle Eastern belly dancers display. I think you get it from growing up eating a lot of hummus and pita bread. This Jeannie had been raised on piroshki; you could see it in her moves. At least we got a chance to ride some camels, which, of course, were trained by Indians. Where the hell were all the locals? Maybe they would come out when the weather got cool. Just waiting for all us foreigners to melt before they showed their faces.

You Give Birth, I'll Videotape

Dubai is a city that has done a great job of branding itself as being very Westerner friendly. So much so that some Americans don't even consider it part of the Middle East. I was doing a radio interview for one of my stand-up shows in Dallas one time and the morning deejays were asking me about my shows in the Middle East. One of the guys said, "I'd be afraid to go to the Middle East. I'd go to Dubai, but the Middle East, I'm not sure about." In all fairness to the guy, maybe he thought it was a sane place in the middle of a crazy place. Kind of like Austin is in Texas.

A lot of Americans are okay with going to Dubai. It's kind of like Cabo to them. What's funny is I've been in the Dubai airport, which is a very international airport, and I've looked around and seen people in all different types of outfits, including the traditional Muslim garb. If someone from America who only knew the Middle East through the perspective of Fox News were dropped into this scene, they would freak out because they'd think they were surrounded by a bunch of al-Qaeda terrorists. When in reality it's just businesspeople, day laborers, and accountants who happen to wear those clothes and once in a while blow things up, assuming they are in the demolitions racket.

After our first trip to Dubai, we were suddenly getting requests to come back every few weeks. The real estate bubble had not burst yet, so there was still a lot of money being thrown around. We would get calls one week before an event with ridiculous offers.

"We want to pay Maz fifty thousand to perform at our event next Tuesday."

My manager at the time was losing his mind. He didn't know how to handle it. We were doing okay in the United States as actors and comedians, but in the Middle East we were superstars. I'm telling you, we were the Brown Collar Comedy Tour. He would get me a ridiculous offer and I would have to remind him that I had a local gig at a university that same night, which obviously paid much less.

"Can we cancel it?" he would ask.

"No, we can't cancel it. The kids have been promoting me for months. I can't flake on them this late."

"Maz, it's fifty grand!"

"I hate those damn kids! But I can't do it. I can't."

"Fifty grand, Maz!"

"Maybe the kids will buy a lot of DVDs."

One event I was able to make was the launch of a new real estate development company in the summer of 2008. For anyone who has forgotten or was not yet born in 2008, the real estate bubble did, in fact, burst worldwide right around that time. So launching a real estate company that year was like buying your wife a diamond necklace the night before you catch her in bed with your best friend. These guys went all out and hired me as well as two world-renowned pianists who were flown in from Japan. No expense was spared. I flew out to do the gig with crutches because I had broken my ankle playing soccer the week before. At the time my wife was pregnant with our first child. I remember telling the organizers that if she went into labor, I might have to cancel the show. Everyone was asking why. It's a seventeen-hour flight from Dubai to Los Angeles, so even if I tried to make it in time, geography was working against me. I was discussing this with a young Jordanian driver on the way to the event. Yes, the driver was Jordanian. This was Dubai, so no locals were to be found.

"But Maz, why do you have to be there? Do you deliver the baby? This is the woman's job, not ours. She goes in the room, has the baby, and then you see him afterwards."

That's how a lot of people think of Middle Eastern men—that we are these macho guys with submissive wives—whereas I'm a modern Middle Eastern man who's grown up in the West and who feels it's my responsibility to be in the hospital room when my wife goes into labor, mostly because I'm the main reason she's there to begin with. Also, I want to see the baby the moment he is born because, like other men, I'm curious if he'll have my eyes, and I must be sure he's the same color as me. My father missed my birth. He was out of the country with my uncle who was very sick and needed medical attention in England at the time. Given that I was the first boy of the family, my dad often told me how proud and happy he was when he got the news. A good friend who happened to be a colonel in the Iranian army called him and told him that he'd had a son. My father replied, "Take his balls, place them on your shoulders, and consider yourself promoted to a general!" It sounds much more poetic in the Turkish dialect that my father spoke, but the point is that he was very happy to have a boy. And before any testicle rights organizations begin protesting this book, I just want to clarify that he didn't really mean for his friend to cut off my balls and place them on his shoulders. He was just trying to say that I was so special that by placing my balls on his shoulders his friend would become a general. Okay, that still doesn't sound right. Let's forget that story.

Anyway, I was so into the upcoming birthing experience that I did the un-macho-est thing that a Middle Eastern man can do—I enrolled my wife and me in Lamaze classes. Biggest waste of time and money and macho-ness ever! If your wife asks you to do this, tell her to take your balls, put them . . . No, don't do that. Just spend that money on a nice dinner when she's pregnant and enjoy one of the last peaceful moments you will have together. Because once that baby arrives, you won't see each other for a long time. No sleep, no romance, no breathing together. Just poop, puke, and burping—and that's just your wife.

The day my son was born—a day that I was mercifully not a seventeen-hour plane ride away—the only thing my wife used her breathing for was to yell at me before she kicked me out of the hospital room. Women in labor tend to take it out on their husbands and rightfully so. We just sit there staring at them while they're doing all the work and then when the baby arrives we tell people that "we" had a baby. "We" didn't do crap. She did it all. In order to help the process, though, we hired a doula. The doula and I played good cop/bad cop with my wife. I was the bad cop because no matter what I said or did, it resulted in my wife yelling at me.

"Honey, you want some water?"

"GET OUT!"

"How about a massage?"

"GET THE HELL OUT!"

"Okay, I'm just going to take a walk around the emergency room and see if anyone wants to hear some jokes. Let me know if you want to hear any because I could really cheer you up."

"YOU WANT TO CHEER ME UP? GET THE HELL

OUT! YOU DID THIS TO ME! YOU'RE LUCKY I CAN'T STAND UP. I WOULD KICK YOUR ASS, JOKEY-MAN!"

"I love you, too, dear. Keep up the good work."

The doula, on the other hand, was the good cop. Anything she said my wife listened to.

"You want some water?"

"Yes, Doula."

"How about a massage?"

"Yes, Doula."

"You wanna hear some jokes?"

"You're a comedian, too? You're so amazing, Doula! Please, do tell. I could use some cheering up!"

As I was going in and out of the hospital room trying to appease my wife in the midst of thirty-two hours of labor, it occurred to me that maybe the Jordanian driver knew what he was talking about when he told me to stay out of the room. Ultimately, my wife had a C-section and I was in there to see my son born. It was magical and gross all at the same time, like the first time you French kiss. "Oh, wow! She's got her tongue in my mouth. It feels like a snake. A wet snake that's probably still covered in its last meal. And some phlegm. Yuk!"

Ironically, I returned to Dubai for some shows a year later and ran into a guy who had seen me at the launch for the real estate development company in 2008. He said he had invested two million dollars in the company and within a year it had gone under. He told me that all he got from his investment was the comedy show. He said that was the most expensive comedy show he had ever paid for. I gave him a hug and told him that next time he should just call me directly. I could save him money and do the show for just one million.

There Are No Lefts in Dubai

Dubai grows so fast that it often seems like hotels open before they are ready. If you ever see pictures of Dubai from the 1980s, there's nothing there. Just a lot of sand and a few buildings. Now when you go there it looks like the skyline of Las Vegas, buildings among buildings among more buildings. A few times, the hotels I stayed at were brand new but little things wouldn't work. The hot water would come out cold; the cold would come out hot; flushing the toilet would start the shower; turning on the shower would call room service; turning on the lights in the bathroom would launch an attack on Bahrain. I wondered if they just clipped the ribbon and figured they'd work out the kinks later. One thing you begin to see in the region is that when it comes to city planning, there aren't a lot of rules and regulations. People get contracts based on relationships, then they just start building and figuring it out as they go.

"I'm building a two-bedroom condo, but it might turn out to be a thirty-story hotel, depending on when the bricks run out." It's gotten better now, but back in 2007–2008 the kinks were definitely still being worked out.

On one trip, the hotel we were staying at was built, but there was no road leading *to* the hotel. Our cab driver kept going in circles trying to get us to the front door. He would get us close and then the road would veer to the right.

"Turn left!" I would holler, seeing the hotel drift away.

"Sir, there are no lefts!"

"You mean it's a one-way?"

"No, there is no road to go left. I have been trying to get to this hotel for a year and I can't get there."

I was not fully aware of how lax the rules were until I took my son with me to Dubai in 2010. At the time, he was about a year and a half old. It was one of my favorite trips as he, my wife, and I spent three weeks in the region. I was doing shows, and we had downtime in between to spend together. One day I took him to a playground inside the Dubai mall. He was running around, climbing the play structure, and having a blast. Then he found the slide. When you put your toddler on a slide in the United States, there are rules as to how they're constructed. There are contractors, foremen, laborers—all who know how to properly install slides. Whoever makes these slides in the United States has to put something on the slide to slow the baby down once it gets to the end. Not in Dubai.

As I watched my boy slide down and get launched into the air, like a tiny, twenty-pound projectile, my heart sank. I chased after him and ran up to the people in charge.

"DID YOU SEE MY SON FLY OFF THE SLIDE? WHERE DID HE GO?"

"He is on the third floor, sir. Just take the elevator up. Once you get there, turn right because there are no lefts."

"THIS IS DANGEROUS! IS THIS SLIDE PERMITTED?"

"Yes sir. But it's permitted to be a seesaw!"

Bombing Big in Dubai

On one of my trips to Dubai in 2013 I arrived during Dubai Art Week. This is a cool gathering of artists and exhibitions from around the world. It allowed me to see a side of Dubai I hadn't seen in the past. For once I wasn't in luxury cars going from gigs to fancy after-parties; instead, I was walking around warehouses, checking out cool art and hearing acoustic guitarists play folk music. If you only watched FOX, you would not know that there is, in fact, a lot of art and culture in the Middle East, not just angry bearded dictators and ululating American-flag burners. People from all different backgrounds are exchanging ideas and getting together for festivals and events that we in the United States have no idea are happening. For example, did you know that they have an *Arab Idol*? Okay, not the best example of something cultural, but still, they have singing competitions.

I was scheduled to perform at a big fund-raiser during the festival. Always the clown, never the artist. As often happens at these events I went up last—and ate it! At the time, I was still the Eddie Murphy of Dubai—although other American comedians had gone out to perform and the market was beginning to get competitive. So maybe I wasn't the Eddie Murphy anymore, but rather the Martin Lawrence. The point is that I was still looked at as an international star comedian whom they had brought in to perform at this exclusive event.

There's nothing worse than grand expectations when it comes to performing. The best thing for a performer is when you do a set where no one knows you and they don't know what to expect. That's when you can kill and they come up to you after saying, "I had never heard of you before. You're the funniest comedian I've ever seen!" You walk out thinking your career is going places. *That random person said I'm the funniest person ever. I'll probably have my own show on ABC next week!* The opposite is the worst. When you show up at an event and everyone knows you. "Maz Jobrani! I am a huge fan. I can't wait to see you. I have seen all your clips on YouTube and I paid two hundred and fifty dollars for tonight's fund-raiser just to see you. You are my favorite!" That often sets you up for failure, because no matter what you do, you won't live up to expectations.

I had been built up as the closing act. I was trying to psych myself up that I would do well and everyone would get his money's worth. The night began with an amazing dance troupe that had been flown in from another country. These guys were doing Michael Jackson choreography and balancing themselves on lampposts. This one guy would just hold himself up horizontally, almost like he was floating on air. One of the most amazing things I had ever seen, and also one of the most intimidating. Right away I knew I was in trouble. These people had glistening abs. They were dancing around like their legs were made of rubber. The one dude levitated. I'm a comedian. I don't levitate. If I'm lucky, I might jump up and down onstage at one point to drive home a punch line, but too much jumping might result in a pulled hammy. It was going to be a tough act to follow.

After the dancers there were speakers, a decadent dinner, an auction, dessert by a German chef and his crew of workers who prepared an amazing display as the German yelled orders with his thick accent. "Now add zhe shoooogah! HURRY UP!" A good five hours of the greatest entertainment I had ever witnessed, and then I heard the deejay nonchalantly summon me for the finale: "Give it up for Maz Jobrani!"

I got on the stage and I was staring down at two hundred tired, sugar-high, wrecked faces who had just spent hundreds of thousands of dollars buying art. I maintained composure and launched into my jokes. Right away I was flopping left and right, so I decided to do crowd work.

"I heard there's Kuwaiti royalty here tonight. Where is he?"

Everyone looked uncomfortable as they pointed to a lady I recognized. I felt like an idiot because when I met her earlier, no one had said, "Maz, this is Princess So and So from Kuwait." I guess they figured that I would know she was a princess, but I had no idea. All I could muster up was an, "Oh yes, of course. Hello Your Highness . . . Excellency . . . Holiness." I never know what to call royalty, so I try to cover all bases.

My next target was an older Indian gentleman in the back of the room whom the auctioneer had spoken to earlier. This man was very dapper, and I figured he must be an artist of some kind. Since my wife is Indian I have some jokes about Indians and their names. I asked the gentleman his name and he replied. I couldn't understand a word he said since he was so far back, and I kept asking him to repeat himself. Now the crowd was getting antsy. Finally I did my Indian jokes and got a lukewarm response. I later was told that this guy was one of the biggest stars in Bollywood. Think the Indian Morgan Freeman. So now I had insulted two famous people by not knowing who they were. I was really starting to seem like the stupid American in the room.

There were a handful of Lebanese in attendance, and they are usually good laughers. So my last attempt at saving myself was my tried and true arsenal of Lebanese jokes. Like how in Lebanon you can actually get a loan from a bank for plastic surgery. They have guys walking into banks saying, "Yes, hello, I am here for a loan. I was going to remodel my house, but I've decided to remodel my wife. We were going to add a bathroom, but we've decided to add some tits." This joke would usually kill in front of a Lebanese crowd, but that night, in front of the princess from Kuwait, not a peep. Even the Lebanese had lost their will to laugh. And when the Lebanese aren't laughing, you're screwed. You just keep yapping away waiting for a spattering of chuckles to end on and get off. You sweat, you ruin your expensive suit, you question why you ever got into this comedy racket in the first place. Then you rush off, make your way to the bar, and find a few allies who enjoyed watching you squirm. You try to downplay it, but they remind you, "Hey, man, you did it the Dubai way. You didn't just bomb. You bombed big."

Beirut, Lebanon

Beirut is like no other place in the world. On one of my trips there, the hotel I was staying at had a Sunday afternoon club—drinks, girls in bikinis, guys with nipple rings, techno music blaring out of the speakers. You would have thought you were in South Beach. Just as I got comfortable and forgot I was in what had been a war zone a few years earlier, I saw three armored tanks roll by, and I suddenly remembered—I was in Beirut.

Things work differently there. The beauty of Beirut is how resilient its people are. The Lebanese would tell us about the civil war they had that lasted for years, followed by the occasional wars and skirmishes and standoffs with Israel. Everyone had stories. One of our promoters was a woman about my age who relayed to me how Bill Cosby once saved her life. Back in the 1980s, in the midst of the civil war, she and her family always made sure to watch *The Cosby Show* together. One night, when the fighting escalated, they went to an underground bunker near their house to avoid the bombings. At a certain point her father realized that it was time for *The Cosby Show* to begin. He told the family to leave the bunker so they could all watch together. A few minutes later, a bomb fell on the bunker; her life was saved by the Cos. As a comedian, I had big shoes to fill in Beirut.

Double-O Maz

The Lebanese are known for partying. In the Middle East and, for that matter, around the world, you will always see them owning nightclubs and restaurants and organizing parties. I think the country has known so much war and strife that the people have just gotten used to it. At some point they decided they could either be dragged down by the conflicts or rise above and celebrate life. The Lebanese have chosen the latter. I was told that during their civil war, they would plan in advance where to set up parties in case fighting broke out in the main part of town—much different priorities than in your amateur war zones. Typically, when the bombs start flying, people go into bunkers and hide until it's over. Not in Lebanon. Instead of hiding, the Lebanese simply move the party into the mountains.

The first time I was in Lebanon the Lebanese Parliament was having trouble agreeing on a new president. This was a political emergency, but if war wasn't going to halt the parties, a minor issue like this wouldn't either. One night at our show at the Casino du Libon (yes, there are casinos in the Middle East) a former Miss Lebanon was in the audience.

"In Lebanon you guys say, 'We have agreed on a Miss

Lebanon,'" I told the audience in welcoming her. "'Who needs to agree on a president? Let's party!'"

The crowd erupted in applause. They were proud of their lust for life and not worried about their political situation. After all, when you've seen years of war, a little disagreement over who's going to be in charge of planning future wars is no big deal.

One of the more politically powerful groups in Lebanon is Hezbollah. Hezbollah, which translated means "the Party of God," is a Shiite Muslim organization whose main supporter is the country of Iran. I was born in Iran, so to someone who is a member of Hezbollah I would be considered an ally. Being Iranian in Hezbollah territory is a good thing, and even though I have an American passport it still says where I was born in the passport. This came in handy at the airport in Beirut, which is run by Hezbollah.

Whenever the passport control guys would see I was born in Iran, a little shimmer would come into their eyes. They'd give me a knowing nod as if to say, "Welcome brother! I am sure you have brought us some bazookas from your country of Iran. We will make the drop when the time is right." I did not want to disappoint, so I would smile back and mumble in broken Arabic, "Salaam alaikum," which means "hello." But my "salaam alaikum" was meant to also convey, "Yes, I have the bazookas. I will make delivery as soon as you stamp my passport and let me in."

I don't know why passport control in almost every country is set up to make you nervous. Do these guys watch episodes of *Homeland* in preparation for work every day? For whatever reason I always feel nervous and, depending on where I am, I try to show my allegiance to them and their country in any way possible. When I land in the United States it's a hearty, "What's up, sir? Good to be back stateside." I can even muster up a southern drawl if need be. In Lebanon, *"Salaam alaikum, habibi!"* (*"habibi"* means "dear"). When I'm in Sweden: "Hello my fancy blond friend. Big fan of the Swedish Chef and Björn Borg!"

The first time I went to Saudi Arabia, I had to be prepared to lie to the guys at passport control. They did not allow live public performances in Saudi, so you were not permitted into the country on a performer's visa. We basically had a prince who supported what we were doing and instructed us to tell the passport guys that we were consultants coming in to consult on something. I was never briefed as to what, exactly, we were consulting on, but it was something big, and very important, and we were going to consult the hell out of it. As I approached the passport guy, I could feel the back of my shirt getting drenched with sweat. My nerves were getting the best of me. What if they figured out my real reason for being there and arrested me? I had heard on Fox News that they cut off your hands for stealing in Saudi Arabia. What would they do if they found out you were planning on telling jokes? Illegally! Maybe they would cut off my tongue. Maybe they would cut off my tongue and hands so I couldn't hold a microphone again! I felt like the guy in the beginning of *Midnight Express* when he's trying to sneak heroin out of Turkey. Except I was trying to sneak jokes into Saudi Arabia.

I hate lying to authorities to begin with, and this was Saudi Arabia, where said authorities were probably just waiting for fibbers so they could make an example out of me. I could see the headline: "Iranian-American Jokester Attempts to Make Joke Out of Anti-Joking Laws." I was just hoping they would see the American passport and not bother asking too many questions. As I approached, there was a British guy on the other side going through passport control at the same time. When the Saudis saw his nationality, both my passport control guy and the guy doing the paperwork for the British guy perked up and said in broken English, "British?"

"Yes," the man answered.

"James Bond!"

"No, I'm not James Bond."

"Yes, yes, James Bond!"

"No, no. Really, I am not James Bond."

"Yes, British. James Bond."

I don't know why these guys were so impressed to see a British dude, but I encouraged it. I figured if they were busy being starstruck by a fake James Bond—who was wearing prescription glasses and carrying a leather dossier—then they'd let me slip right through. I could have easily pointed out the un-James-Bond-like qualities of this guy: "Bond has twenty-twenty vision and would never carry a case like that. He also has better teeth than this guy and is well built. This guy is too skinny to be Bond. He looks more like Mr. Bean."

Instead I smiled at my passport agent and agreed with him. "James Bond," I said.

He understood. "Oh yes, James Bond."

I even started speaking in broken English to blend in. "Yes, yes. I say him James Bond."

As the agent looked longingly at the retreating double agent, he quickly stamped my passport and let me through. Saved by 007!

Conversely, the worst experiences I've ever had going through passport control always occur in Kuwait. For some reason every time I've gone there, they've detained me and asked extra questions. I don't know why, but I'm told that Kuwait does not get along with

Iran. So a typical experience at passport control in Kuwait, for me, might go like this. The guy will see my American passport and say,

"American? Great!"

Then he will look inside and see the place of my birth,

"Born in Iran? Wait! What is your father's name?"

"My father passed away. His name was Khosro."

"What is your grandfather's name?"

"Well he passed away even before, but his name was Jabbar."

The whole time I'm thinking, *How far back are we going with this thing? Is this passport control or Ancestry.com?*

One time it seemed like Inspector Clouseau would keep going: "What is your great-grandfather's name? What was HIS great-grandfather's name? And his? And his? Has anyone in your family ever been named Moishe? I knew it! You're Jewish!" Fortunately, he just looked at me and simply said, "You wait. I be back."

Whenever they say that to me—"You wait. I be back"—I always get nervous and start fidgeting. I had not done anything, but I also didn't know what kind of crap my grandfather might have been into. I thought Clouseau might come back and say, "Your grandfather has a parking violation from ninety-seven years ago. He was parked in a handicap camel parking zone. It is way overdue. You owe us two million dollars!"

Ironically, whenever you're *leaving* a country, the folks at passport control and security don't seem to be as concerned. I remember leaving Kuwait once, and the same country that had given me a full interrogation coming in didn't even care what I had in my bags as I left. I put my backpack on the conveyor belt and went through the metal detector. As I went through I noticed that instead of observing the contents of my bag, the security guy was busy checking out the ass of the lady who was in front of me in line. I could've been walking through with a Kalashnikov and he could have cared less. He was more concerned with getting a peek than stopping me from hijacking a plane. Who knew that all al-Qaeda had to do to hijack a plane was start working with Kim Kardashian.

Anyway, back in Lebanon, passing through the Beirut airport I was Iranian-ing myself up as much as possible. "Salaam! Salaam!" Hand to my chest in respect with a slight bow and a smile. A look in my eyes as if to say, "I've got the weapons. I've got plenty and plenty of weapons." The whole time I was sweating, praying they did not look me up on YouTube and see all my jokes making fun of the Iranian leadership. "Do you guys have WiFi at the airport? Because if you do, I just recommend that you never watch anything on YouTube. You can never trust anything you see on there. All doctored videos. Total American propaganda."

Funny Shiite Coming Sunni

Lebanon is a country of contradictions. You have so many different political factions and religions that it would take a Ph.D. in political science to understand them. Fortunately, I had a few months of Ph.D. education under my belt. There are Christians and Druze and Sunni Muslims and Shiite Muslims and a million other groups in Lebanon. This makes it particularly hard when you're a comedian who likes to work the crowd and build jokes around the audience.

Now here's a little secret for comedy fans: A lot of times when we do crowd work, the jokes we seem to come up with on the fly are jokes we've used a thousand times. But sometimes that can start to feel a bit hacky, so I actually like it when I'm given something unexpected from the audience. I did a show one time in New York and a guy in the audience was named Osama Hussein. Yes, this poor fellow had the first name of Osama bin Laden and the last name of Saddam Hussein. What are the chances? That's like being named Adolf Mussolini during World War II, or like being a Red Sox fan named DiMaggio Mantle. The only way it could've gotten worse is if his middle name were Kim Jong-il—Osama Kim Jong-il Hussein. So obviously, when Osama Hussein comes to your show, you've just been gifted five minutes of new material by the comedy gods. Just the time it takes to inspect his ID to make sure he's legit takes a good two or three minutes.

In Lebanon, this doesn't always happen. That's because there are a lot of Christian Lebanese and they do not have the types of names that will help with your act. One time I was in Beirut doing a show on top of a bar. That's not a misprint—I was performing a stand-up comedy routine on top of a bar where patrons drink alcohol, just like in the movie *Coyote Ugly*. I had just done some shows in Saudi Arabia the night before, where drinking is strictly prohibited, and now I was in Beirut, where not only was drinking allowed, but they had me standing in front of a hundred bottles of alcohol telling jokes. Before I went up, the club manager asked if I wanted anything to drink.

"You wouldn't happen to have any tequila?" I inquired.

The Lebanese are proud people. The manager responded confidently. "Of course we have tequila. Why wouldn't we have tequila?"

"Would you happen to have Don Julio?"

The manager, feeling challenged: "Of course we have Don Julio. Why wouldn't we have Don Julio?"

"Can I have a double shot of Don Julio on the rocks?"

Manager, now cocky: "You will have a whole bottle!"

"No, no," I said, worried. "I don't need a whole bottle."

"This is Lebanon. You're getting a whole bottle!"

And so a bottle of Don Julio was designated as my personal bottle for the evening and brought to me in the manager's office, where I was feeling fairly smug about things. Eat that, Bill Cosby.

Now, I don't like being drunk onstage. If I ever drink during a show, it's usually one glass that I will sip during my set. But this was Lebanon and I was telling jokes on top of a bar, so things worked differently. I went onstage . . . I mean I went on a bar with my glass of Don Julio, leaving the bottle behind. At a certain point I decided to riff on a joke about how hard it is to travel being a Middle Easterner and asked a guy in the audience his name. I was expecting Ahmed or Mohammad or Ali—something I could work with. Instead the guy had the most common name ever.

"Joseph."

"Joseph? As in Joey?" I asked.

"Yes."

"Is that a made-up name?"

"No. It is my given name."

"Oh, okay. Then your friend there, what's his name?"

"Anthony."

"As in Tony?"

"Yes."

"And the guy next to him?"

"Vincent."

"As in Vinny? What are you guys, the Sopranos?"

"No," he said without a hint of a smile. "We're Christian."

Buying time, I reached for the tequila and took a sip. I hadn't noticed, but I had worked my way to the bottom of the glass as I struggled to turn the joke. Soon enough, a waiter showed up with another glass. I think the manager saw that I was struggling a bit and decided to send me more inspiration. Besides, this was Lebanon, and it *was* my bottle for the night; he wanted to make sure I finished it.

There I was with two double glasses of Don Julio warming my belly, standing on a bar in Beirut, trying to figure out my next move when I noticed a group of women in the corner laughing, talking, and completely ignoring me as if I weren't standing on a bar with microphone in hand.

"Excuse me, ladies. What's going on here?"

They were screaming and yelling. "Bachelorette party!" one of them shouted, indicating I should stop bothering them.

"Bachelorette party? We have a stand-up comedy show going on."

More hollering. "Whatever, dude."

"No, ladies, this is an advertised show. These hundred and fifty people staring up at the bar have paid to see me perform. You have to keep it down."

"Woo-hoo!" they hollered. "Keep it down!"

"No, you're not supposed to yell 'Woo-hoo, keep it down' at me. I'm telling *you* to keep it down."

More screaming and shouting, and I'm on the verge of losing control.

"Why is the bachelorette wearing a penis balloon on her head? This poor girl is getting married. She's got many years of humiliation ahead of her. Don't make her wear the penis balloon."

"Penis balloon!" they hollered. It was clear they did not understand why I was standing on the bar. Everything I said, they repeated. They thought I was leading them in cheers instead of performing stand-up.

Another sip of tequila. A new glass arrived.

To recap: For a comedian who does Middle Eastern jokes, names like Joey, Tony, and Vinny can really throw you for a loop. Add to that the fact that you're performing on a bar, sipping your third glass of a double tequila, and engaging in call and response with a bachelorette party, and it can cause real confusion. Was I in Beirut or Las Vegas?

Making things worse, a man who was the chaperone for the bachelorette party approached the stage—which, have I mentioned, was just a bar?—and asked me in broken English when I was going to be finished telling my stories. It seemed the women were getting restless and had heard enough of me babbling into a microphone. They wanted dance music to get the party started. He actually interrupted me midjoke as 150 people were watching my set.

"You. When you finish?"

"Excuse me?"

"When you stop?"

I checked my watch. "I've got another half hour. This is a comedy show. They paid me to perform tonight."

Obviously a professional in his chosen field, he was prepared to work through such trivial roadblocks. "You sing?"

"Do I sing?"

"When you do some songs?"

"I'm not singing. Me do comedy. Ha-ha. Jokey joke."

"Not funny."

"You barely speak English. How do you know I'm not funny?"

"I know. You not funny."

Great, half loaded on tequila in front of a less than ordinary crowd, I run into the Lebanese Simon Cowell. "So you're a judge of comedy in a language you don't even speak?" I asked. "Go over there and sit down next to the girl with the penis balloon on her head so I can finish my show."

At this point he didn't look too happy with me. I'm not sure if he understood what I was saying, but he seemed upset. He was holding a small bowl of cashews and popping them into his mouth, just crunching the nuts slowly and staring at me. I didn't know if he was going to pull out a gun and shoot me or if he was blitzed out of his head even more than I was.

Trying to lighten the mood, I asked, "What're you eating?"

"Nuts."

"Throw me one."

He reached into the bowl and tossed a cashew in my direction. I was at least five feet above him and the cashew sailed high overhead in what seemed like slow motion. This was risky; in fact, it was the tequila talking. If it had hit me in the eye, or I had somehow reached for it and lost my balance, I would have ended up looking like an idiot. Even worse, I could've fallen off the bar and ended up in a Lebanese hospital. But I kept my composure and somehow snapped the nut out of thin air with my mouth—like a seal at the circus. The audience was impressed: a roaring round of applause. And the chaperone, head hung in defeat, waddled back to the bachelorettes. Bill Cosby NEVER did that!

Making Hezbollah Laugh

I was being exposed to all the different religions and people of the country and at some point someone thought it would be a good idea for me and the Axis of Evil comedians to set up a meeting with Hezbollah leadership and film it. We were in the middle of a five-country tour and had been filming the whole thing to come out with a "behind the scenes" documentary that we would air on Showtime Arabia, a cable network that showed Western programs. Our meeting with Hezbollah would be part of this new format. I guess having three Middle Eastern–American comedians meet with Hezbollah would make good television, right? What nobody thought about was the fact that the United States considers Hezbollah a terrorist organization and would probably not encourage three of its citizens to set up a meeting and film it—even if we were comedians. I can imagine the State Department representative discouraging us.

"Hezbollah is a terrorist organization."

"Yeah, but we're comics, so it's cool."

"They are a TERRORIST ORGANIZATION."

"We just want to talk to them. Maybe tell a few jokes."

"THEY ARE TERRORISTS! THEY WILL KIDNAP YOU!"

"We understand that, but do you think they will laugh at our jokes? Kidnappers have to laugh too, right?"

The person making the introductions told us that our "fixer" would meet us in the parking lot of a grocery store to take us to the meeting with Hezbollah. Anytime you hear the word "fixer" in the Middle East, there is cause to be nervous. In Los Angeles, where I live, a fixer is someone who comes to your house and fixes the washing machine. In foreign countries, a fixer is a guy who is connected and can get you into seedy situations. As we waited for our fixer, I had a feeling he wouldn't be showing up with a tool belt.

The other comedians and I were waiting in two cars in a grocery store parking lot; the fixer was running late. The more we waited, the more nervous I became. I kept thinking of the opening scene of *The Insider* with Russell Crowe, in which the Al Pacino character sets up a meeting with Hezbollah and they throw a burlap sack over his head and rush him to the rendezvous with guns drawn. I felt like we were about to be given the same burlap sack treatment. I told one of the Axis comics that this is how every bad kidnapping movie begins—with the victims waiting in a parking lot, in the back of a van, to meet the bad guys. What had seemed like an interesting idea when we were first presented with it was beginning to feel like a really, really bad idea. Also, it was a sunny day. The last thing I wanted was to not be able to enjoy the great weather because I had a burlap sack over my head.

Eventually our Hezbollah fixer showed up and he wasn't what I expected at all. I was expecting a guy in Fidel Castro military fatigues, maybe with a couple of sidekicks carrying Kalashnikovs. Or maybe a guy in a full Muslim dishdasha with some prayer beads in his hands. You know . . . the outfit. Instead, our guy looked like an employee right out of Ed Hardy—designer jeans, T-shirt, gelled hair, even a cigarette hanging out of his mouth. He told us to follow him to Hezbollah territory where we would meet the "main guy."

The only thing worse than the fixer in these situations is the main guy. The van I was in followed the fixer's car; one of the guys from our team who was an Algerian Shiite rode with the fixer. The closer we got to Hezbollah territory the more our driver, who was a Christian Lebanese, kept complaining in broken English. "This no good. This no good." It's never a good thing when a local is telling you that he's getting nervous. It would be the equivalent of me driving some guests around Los Angeles and once we got to a bad strip mall, just completely freaking out: "This is the worst stretch of shopping in California! There are just no good restaurants for miles! We could starve and die. Or eat something full of saturated fat!" You're the local. You're supposed to keep your cool. But our driver wasn't holding back. Even when he spoke Arabic, which we didn't understand, we could make out that he was nervous.

"*Blakha blakha blakha* BURLAP SACK *blakha blakha blakha* HOSTAGE!"

Meanwhile, ahead in the fixer's car, our Algerian friend quickly figured out that the fixer was also a drug dealer, reaching this conclusion when the fixer offered to sell us drugs. I think the fixer did not completely understand who the hell we were. He'd just heard "Americans" and thought we'd probably want to buy some drugs from him. Or maybe he heard "comedians" and thought we would want to buy some drugs from him. Either way, he had drugs and was offering to sell us some.

I've come to learn that our fears of people in other parts of the world are usually a bit overblown. The real thing that most of our "enemies" want is simply to have some of our money taking up space inside their pockets. I remember when the "War on Terror" originally began and the military was looking for Osama bin Laden in the mountains of Afghanistan. There was a newspaper article about how the U.S. military had given a satellite phone to a warlord and told him that if he saw bin Laden he should use the phone to call the military. The warlord had agreed, and no sooner had the U.S. military packed up their Humvees than the warlord set up a phone system where his tribesmen could use the satellite phone to call their families in other countries and he would charge them to use the phone. The U.S. military had thought this guy was interested in catching bin Laden like they were, when he was just interested in setting up a for-profit long distance phone service. We wanted justice, he wanted to be AT&T.

So let's recap: I, a born Shiite Muslim who's not really religious, am in one car with Aron Kader, one of the Axis comedians whose father is Palestinian and mother is Mormon. We are being driven by a paranoid Lebanese Christian who thinks we're going to get kidnapped. Another Axis comedian, Ahmed Ahmed, who is Egyptian and Sunni Muslim, is in a second car with another Christian Lebanese driver who's freaking out as well. A third car has our Algerian Shiite Muslim friend with a Hezbollah fixer who's trying to sell him some hash. There's a country of Jews just an hour away and a warlord in Afghanistan selling airtime. Meanwhile, somewhere there's a State Department guy who thinks we listened to him. "Good thing they took my advice and didn't go to meet up with Hezbollah. If they had they would be in grave danger at this very moment. By my estimates they would have had their hands cut off by now and be watching as they were fed to goats." All caught up?

Aron Kader and I were beyond nervous in our car. In the other car our Algerian friend was making excuses to get us out of the potential drug deal, as we got closer and closer to our meeting spot in the heart of Hezbollah territory. We were in a busy neighborhood with shops and families walking around as dusk arrived. There was probably no real reason to be afraid, but the buildup, combined with our nervous driver, had us completely paranoid. The fixer told us he was going to take us into some building where we would meet our guy. That's when our Algerian friend called the whole thing off. He told the fixer that we were running late for our show that night and that we would try to set up another meeting on another day. Don't call us, we'll call you.

As we all sped away in our van, our Algerian friend, who was now riding with us, told us why he had gotten nervous—he started thinking that the guy we were meeting might have been more of a low level criminal than a member of Hezbollah's political party.

He didn't want us to go to this meeting and end up getting kidnapped not for political reasons, but for a ransom. So our meeting with Hezbollah was called off. Part of me was relieved, but part of me was bummed. We were on the verge of telling Hezbollah some jokes. We were going to make them laugh. We were going to make it on Hezbollah's Top 10 Comics to Watch list. We were going to bring peace to the Middle East. At the least, that must be worth a development deal for your own TV show: *Hezbollafeld.*

Later that night when we did our show I was nervous. I figured we must be on Hezbollah's radar now that we had stood them up. And who knew how they took being stood up. Maybe it was a huge insult. "No one stands up Hezbollah! How dare they? The comedians must die!" Also, and more importantly, given that Hezbollah's biggest financial supporter is the government of Iran and the fact that I did jokes making fun of the Iranian regime, I was worried about doing those jokes in Lebanon. As I performed in front of a thousand people in Beirut, I began to pace quickly back and forth onstage when I got to the jokes about Iran. I figured if someone from Hezbollah had been sent to shut me up with a bullet, they would have a tougher time hitting a moving target. For good measure I pondered doing some jokes that would require me to do somersaults as well. I don't know if anyone was sent to kill me that night, but I finished my set with no bullets flying and all appendages intact. It's always a good show when no one gets shot or maimed. Especially you.

Finding Out I'm a Hooker

When you perform in Beirut, you have to go to a government office a few days into your trip and they ask you if the promoter is treating you right. I've never experienced that anywhere else, but I'm guessing it's because there are a lot of shady promoters and the government wants to make sure that they're not taking advantage of acts that come to Beirut. When our promoter told us that one of us comedians would have to get up at nine o'clock in the morning to go to this office, I took the responsibility. They told me that even when Phil Collins came there a few years earlier, one of his bandmates had to get up early in the morning to make this trip and confirm that Phil and company were being treated properly.

I was a big fan of Phil Collins as a kid—even before I knew I was going to be bald like him. I always thought I would lose my virginity to the song "In the Air Tonight." I know it's cheesy, but what a great song to lose it to. Especially if you can time your orgasm to the drum solo. I don't remember what song I lost my virginity to, or if there was even any music playing in the background. And if I was able to control my orgasms to time them to any drum solo I probably would be in a different line of work. At any rate, the fact that Phil Collins had been expected to check in with this office made me want to do it, too. Granted, Phil had sent some roadie from his band, but still, we were kindred souls. Two artists who had visited Beirut. Two bald brothers on a journey to entertain the world. Two guys who could've shared the sanctity of a drum solo had I been able to control my bodily functions with a bit more accuracy.

I figured I would go into this office, sign a piece of paper, and then be on my way. However, once I entered, I was surrounded by a bunch of women who looked like Russian prostitutes. I asked the promoter what band the prostitutes were with and she told me that they were brought into the country as "dancers." I thought, *Wow, these dancers are dressed in their full skimpy dance outfits at nine o'clock in*

Amman, Jordan

When the Axis of Evil Comedy Tour special came out on Comedy Central, we began getting e-mails from around the country. This was in early 2007, and our YouTube comedy videos were becoming popular. I knew things were getting hot when I kept getting my own clips e-mailed to me more times than I cared to. I was getting fed up—with myself: "Doesn't this guy have any new material? 'Persian, like the cat, meow!' I get it. Now write some new stuff." Critics aside, people were beginning to know us. Some congratulated us. Some asked when we would be performing near their hometowns. Others just assumed we were al-Qaeda operatives using YouTube to disseminate our propaganda.

If I had been asked where I thought we might be performing outside the United States a year after the special aired, I would have responded England, Canada, Australia—any English-speaking country. I never in a thousand years would have said Jordan. Yet as we began to grow in popularity, that very call arrived.

"Hello. Yes. We would like to have you come do your show in Jordan."

"Oh, well, thank you very much for the invitation, bro," I responded. "But our shows are actually in English, so I'm not sure you guys would get it."

"But I'm speaking English to you right now, you idiot."

"Um, yeah, that's a good point."

I was guilty of stereotyping an entire nation. Many of the people in the Middle East speak English very well and know our culture in great depth. The rest of the world knows a lot more about America than Americans know about the rest of the world. In Jordan, you can do a joke about Lindsay Lohan and they'll get it: "Oh, that Lindsay . . . always in the rehab!" They know all our pop culture references, whereas some people in the United States couldn't even name all the different countries in the Middle East. (But they can name all our drug-addicted starlets.) I've heard people say we should just "bomb the whole goddamned region." You tell them that there's different countries out there and they stare at you blankly. You have to wonder how many Americans were dropped on their heads at birth. Either that or they've watched too much Fox News, which is the adult version of being dropped on your head.

The King and I

Once it was confirmed we were going to Jordan to do a show, I received the highest-ranking correspondence of my life. One day, while checking my e-mail, I clicked on something from the Office of His Majesty, King Abdullah II of Jordan. Normally when you get an e-mail from someone named "His Majesty," it's asking you to send him your bank account information so he can wire you millions of dollars he intends to share with you when he leaves his poverty-stricken country for a bright future in America. At first I assumed it was a scam. Adding to my doubts was the brevity of the note: His Majesty, the e-mail said, wished to have my mailing address. Things moved quickly from doubt to worry.

"Oh shit. Now I've pissed off the king of Jordan. And he's coming to get me!"

These Arabs don't mess around. I sat sifting through my old material, trying to figure out which joke he'd taken offense to. Was it the one where I made fun of how Arabs talk fast, as if they're perpetually on cocaine? Why did they need my mailing address? Did they really think I'd just give it to them? How stupid was their intelligence service?

"Yes, hello, we would like to kill you. Can you please give us your address so we know where to find you?"

I wasn't falling for that one. You've got to get up pretty early in the morning to trick this Iranian-American comedian. Like any good spy with a hit out on him, I did my research to see what this was all about. I felt like Jason Bourne in *The Bourne Identity* trying to determine who the good guys were and who the bad guys were. No one was to be trusted. I contacted the other Axis of Evil comedians to bend their ears, but I had to be careful. For all I knew, they could be in on "the plot"—double-secret-agent comedians. I broached the topic carefully.

"Hey, it's Maz. Just calling to say hello. Has anything weird happened to you lately?"

"Weird! I'll tell you what's weird," one of the panicked

comedians shout-whispered into the phone. It sounded as though he hadn't slept in days. "I got an e-mail from the king of Jordan asking for my mailing address! I think he's trying to kill me!"

Now we both were panicked. This was a bigger conspiracy than I originally thought. Turns out we had all gotten the same e-mail. It appeared that the Jordanians planned to take out all four of us before the Axis of Evil Comedy Tour really got its momentum going. Just like the president and vice president, it was imperative—for the future of comedy, as well as our own lives—that we not appear in the same place at the same time, lest we make it easy on the assassins. We had to think quickly. How were we going to dodge this? Should we just pack our bags and move to Brazil without even saying anything to our families or booking agents? Should we rename the tour and try to keep touring under the radar? The Axis of Not So Evil Comedy Tour? The Kinder Gentler Axis of Evil Comedy Tour? Or The Don't Shoot Us, We're Just Comedians Tour? Whatever we were going to do we had to decide fast because His Majesty was waiting for our reply. I'm fairly certain that if you take too long to reply to someone named His Majesty, that will just make the impending death that much more violent.

We were nervous. We were scared. We came up with a plan that only dumb comedians thinking the king of Jordan has time to assassinate them would contrive. Ahmed Ahmed, the Egyptian of the group, had a P.O. box. Apparently he'd had other kings come after him in the past, so he was better prepared than the rest of us.

"Let's give the king of Jordan that address," I suggested. "That way, if he wants to mail us a bomb, he'll just kill the mailbox guy."

Ahmed sent them his P.O. box address. A few days later, we received letters on His Majesty's official letterhead. The gist of it was, "I saw your Axis of Evil comedy special and really enjoyed it.

Thank you for doing what you're doing. It is helping break stereotypes of Middle Easterners in the West."

I was in shock. Was this all part of a more diabolical plot? Was he trying to trick us into letting down our guard before coming after us? Upon conferring with the other Axis guys, we concluded—not just because it was true, but also because the stress of being hunted was taking its toll—that this was actually a very nice and sincere letter from the king of Jordan. It was the most amazing letter I had ever gotten. And to think my mother wanted me to be a lawyer. Hah! If I had been a lawyer I never would have gotten a letter from a king! Maybe a magistrate, but who wants a letter from a magistrate? What the hell is a magistrate anyway? Try explaining that term to my mom. "You got letter from a magistrate? Is that a magician who is eh-straight? I thought all magicians vere gay!"

Of course, one of the first people I told about the letter was my mom. Telling your Iranian mother that a king has written a personal letter to you saying that he enjoys your comedy is one of the best ways to finally get her off your back and accept that you have made the right career choice. That said, never underestimate a Persian mother's persistence.

"Mom, guess what? I just got a letter from the king of Jordan. He loves my comedy."

"Really?"

"Yes, really."

"Dat's nice."

"That's *nice*?"

"Vhat else did he say?"

"Nothing. Just that he saw it on DVD and enjoyed it."

"So nothing else came in deh letter?"

"What else should have come in the letter?"

"He is a king. Gold? Cash? A virgin?"

"No gold, no cash, no virgins."

"Vhat kind of king is he? Tell me vhen deh king of Kuwait writes you. He vill definitely send a virgin. Perobably vearing gold and carrying cash."

People wouldn't know this, but the king of Jordan is actually a really cool dude. He was educated in the West and is very big on showing a positive image of Middle Easterners, Arabs, and Muslims throughout the world. He is also a fan of Western film and TV. As a matter of fact, he was an extra in an episode of *Star Trek* a while back. You can find the clip on YouTube. Just enter "king of Jordan *Star Trek*." He's the guy in the background as the scene begins. That's right—the king of Jordan is a Trekkie! How many other kings do you know who are Trekkies? I can see him attending a Star Trek convention and mingling with the other Trekkies.

"I see your name tag says 'king of Jordan,'" someone might say, and then very dramatically add: "I, too, am a king. The king of Planet Barzan."

"No, I'm actually the real king of Jordan."

"And I am the real king of Planet Barzan."

"Yes, but your planet is fictional. I'm king of a real country on Planet Earth."

"Greetings, earthling!"

"I'm not just an average earthling. I'm a king."

"I, too, am a king. King of the Planet Barzan!"

"Maybe I'll just go switch my nametag to something else."

The Jordanian Distribution Deal

When we arrived in Jordan, the promoters told us that the shows were sold out. Amman is a bustling city with a good mix of East and West. It has some great restaurants and nightclubs, as well as some historical sites. Parts of the city are built vertically, and one of my favorite activities was sitting at an outdoor café, overlooking the city, and sipping tea while the afternoon call to prayer went out. It was awe inspiring and somehow soothing. If only Fox News cameras could have seen me then. They would probably report me as a terrorist taking a break from his daily terrorist activities and sipping on peppermint terrorist tea. It's all about perspective, I guess.

I was surprised that the shows were all sold out so far in advance. This was the first time we were in the region, and I had no idea enough people even knew who we were to sell ten seats. I asked the promoter how it happened.

"Have that many people seen us online?"

"Oh no, Maz, most people have seen the actual DVD."

"I didn't know we had a distribution deal in Jordan."

"Of course you do. One person bought it and everyone saw it. It's called a Jordanian distribution deal. Also known as a bootleg."

It's amazing how pervasive bootlegging is in the Middle East. There's a reason why they know so much about American culture. We actually visited a store in the center of Amman that was all bootlegs and nobody seemed to care. Whereas in the United States the guys selling bootlegs have to sell on bedsheets on street corners so they can quickly pack up and outrun police, this guy had an official store. He had bootlegs of every American film and TV program ever made. If you wanted *Seinfeld*, he had it. If you wanted

The Fast and the Furious, he had all 243 installments of the franchise. Even if you wanted a TV series that had been canceled years ago, it was there. At the time he had our Axis of Evil DVD displayed prominently in the front of the store. When he first saw us coming in, he freaked out because he thought we would be upset. But I was flattered that the guy had bootlegged us. To be on Comedy Central was one thing. But to be robbed by a Jordanian bootlegger meant we'd really arrived. I walked up to the guy, gave him a hug, and thanked him. Then I asked him how much our masterpiece cost.

"A dollar."

"Just one dollar? Are you kidding me?"

"Fine, give me fifty cents. You got a deal, my friend."

"No, I'm not trying to buy it."

"Then why are you asking the price?"

"I'm just saying—it's kind of a hit. Don't you think you could get a little more money for it? How about two dollars?"

"Two dollars? Who do you think you are? *The Fast and the Furious?*"

The King Arriveth

Something special happened in Amman. We got a message from the king's people that he might be attending a show. Of course, we were nervous he would end up flaking out at the last minute. After all, he's the king of a country. He must have more important things to do than attend a comedy show. And yet, the night before the show we got a message that a "special guest" would be there and that no filming would be permitted. It was official—the king of Jordan, His Majesty, would be coming to see us perform live.

I was excited and nervous at the same time. What if he came

and I had a bad set? Bombing in front of a crowd of drunk tourists at one o'clock in the morning was one thing, but bombing in front of a king was a whole different demoralizing matter. How would I ever recover from something like that? Would they even allow me back into Jordan if I had a bad set? It's amazing how a comedian's mind works. No matter how long we've been doing it or how good we get, when we are faced with big shows we have a fear something will go wrong. The key is after years of doing it, you learn to lower the stakes and just have fun. If the crowd doesn't get your humor then you break from your set and do crowd work. If they still don't give you any love, then you barrel through the set and grab a drink afterward. No matter what happens, the clock keeps ticking and after twenty or thirty minutes you'll be offstage and life goes on.

All this is much easier said than done, especially when you have a king in your audience. For some reason I kept imagining a firing squad. And you can't really enjoy a drink if you've got a bunch of holes in your body.

I kept convincing myself it was like any other show. Sure he's a king, but he's still a human being. He puts on his pants one leg at a time, just like everyone else. Although I'm sure he has someone else put his pants on for him, so maybe he's different in that way. But he wears pants, just like everyone else. Yet his pants are probably lined with gold, so okay, he's better in that way, too. The point is that he's a person. Yes, that's the point. He's a person with pants and there's nothing to fear. Except that he has an army, and they all have their own pants, too. And if he didn't like the jokes, he could order them to shoot me. My mother was right—I should've been a lawyer.

My nerves were getting to me. I was accustomed to being the closer on our tour, which meant I would always perform last.

Usually I would show up at the start of the show to wish the others good luck and then sit in the green room waiting my turn. This was difficult because I would amp up at the start of the show and then pace back and forth like a caged lion, waiting for my turn and losing patience. The night the king was coming, I didn't need this extra stress.

Just before the show was set to begin, I glanced out my hotel window to check on the crowds. The night before, there had been a long line of cars waiting to valet park. But that night, there were no cars. Instead there were soldiers who had closed the street down for the king's arrival. I tried to calm down and watch some TV, but as soon as I sat down there were sirens. A bunch of SUVs led by a police escort arrived at the venue: the king and his motorcade. Before the cars had even stopped, guys in secret service suits jumped out and began running up and down in front of the entrance. I was jumping up and down clapping from my hotel window. I had never had a motorcade come to my shows—I was a motorcade virgin! I felt like I was in an episode of 24, and for once I wasn't the bad guy. My heart began pounding. The hair on my arms pricked up. What the hell was I doing still in my hotel room? I should be down there, kneeling on one knee and welcoming His Majesty.

By the time I arrived in the street, the king had already been whisked away to a private room. Only the soldiers with big guns were left, and it was clear they had no idea who I was. For all they knew, I was the guy trying to put a hit on the king, the reason they had to carry around those giant weapons. I wanted to put them at ease so they knew that I was not a threat. I figured I could tell them a joke, then they would set down their giant guns and we'd all have a laugh. Since they wouldn't understand English jokes, I attempted to break the ice with my broken Arabic.

"Salaam alaikum, habibi."

"What's up, bro?"

Holy shit! Even the soldiers spoke English! Are we the only dumb country that encourages our kids NOT to learn other languages? How was I going to speak behind these peoples' backs in front of their faces when they all spoke English so well? The Jordanians weren't making anything easy.

The King Sit Rule

I made my way to the green room and settled in. We had plenty of time to kill before our show started. The night before we had a violinist open for twenty minutes, which was a relaxing way to get in the zone. As I was getting comfortable the promoter came running into the green room.

"Where is Ahmed Ahmed? He is hosting the show, no?"

"Yes, he's hosting, but we still have the twenty minutes of the violinist before we start. He's not here yet. He should be here soon."

"Tonight there will be no violinist! Tonight, the rule is, when the king sits, the show starts!"

"What!" I sprang to my feet. "No violinist?" This was shocking. "What kind of rule is that?"

Apparently it's a rule that dates back to the Roman times. When Caesar sat, the lions ate the gladiators. I always thought that the king would mingle a bit before the show, work the crowd, allow his handlers to get photos of him interacting with the commoners. Maybe have some popcorn, some Raisinets, answer some easy trivia questions displayed on the screen, and then we would start. But I guess it makes sense that they didn't want the king waiting around. After all, he was the king. Of their country. He probably had other things to do than listen to a violin solo while waiting for comedians to tell jokes.

I asked what would happen if the king sat but then decided to stand up. Would we stop the show until he sat again? What if he had static cling on his pants and he kept getting up to straighten them out? What if he had to use the restroom?

"Stop making jokes," the promoter explained to a roomful of comedians. "This is very serious. We have to get Ahmed here right now. The king is almost seated."

The promoter was freaking out. Not only might he lose his job as a promoter if the king was made to wait, he might even be deported. This only made me more nervous. As I said, anytime a local gets nervous in a Middle Eastern country, that's when you should start getting nervous. Usually locals like to sit back and laugh at us Americans for being so scared of everything in the region. But when you see the promoter sweating and begging you to find the show's host, pronto, you know it's serious. We all went for our cell phones at once, placing calls to Ahmed to alert him to this new "King Sit" rule, only to discover that none of our phones worked. The king's security had blocked all cell phones so that no one could use a phone to detonate a bomb. This shit was getting real.

Now the race was on between the king sitting and Ahmed getting out of the shower. I and Aron Kader, the other comedian on tour, began to brainstorm. One of us could host and just bring Ahmed up when he arrived. We would just go on and do as much time as was needed until we had our third comic. It was a wild scramble, and the whole thing was falling apart when Ahmed strolled in, clueless about the mayhem.

"What's up, guys?"

"Where have you been? We're starting!"

"We still got the violinist, right?"

"Wrong!" I hollered, half crazed by now. "The show starts when the king sits!"

"I didn't know that."

"Everyone knows that! It's the King Sit rule!"

Being thrown random King Sit rules before the show made the experience that much more nerve-wracking. We felt as if the rules could be changed at any moment. What if the king decided to do some jokes before the show?

"The king has decided he wants to go on and do five."

"Oh come on. That's bullshit! I was getting ready to go on."

"That's the rule. If the king wants to go on, he goes on. It's his country."

And what if the king went on and ran longer than his allotted five minutes? "He's been up there twenty minutes, man! Give him the light! Give the king the light!"

Would you be allowed to tell the king that you didn't appreciate him taking extra time onstage? "Listen, bro, I know you're the king and all. But that wasn't cool what you did. I'm just telling you a lot of comics don't appreciate it."

"I'm sorry. I didn't see the light."

"That's bullshit, King. You saw the light."

"I swear. I've never worked this room before."

"Oh yeah? Then how come everyone here knows you?"

"Because I am the king."

To our relief, Ahmed went on and the show proceeded without a glitch. This was during the Bush administration, and I had jokes about President Bush as well as the president of Iran, Mahmoud

Ahmadinejad. It's strange performing political material in front of a king because he really could try to do something about whatever issue you're joking about. Every time I would get to those jokes I made sure to look at him with the punch line. As if to say, "Dude, you can do something about this. These are suggestions."

The show went so well that the king invited us to the palace the next day. He was very gracious and complimentary. We were excited to be there and we took pictures with everyone. It's not often you get to be in the palace of a king, so you want proof that you were there. We took pictures with the king, his secretary, some random dude who might have been a bodyguard or someone's brother. I wanted anything I could get my hands on to prove this was happening. I asked if they had mugs, key chains, maybe some gold. In the end we had to settle on the pictures as our only proof. I could anticipate my mom's reaction already: "You vent all deh vay to deh guy's palace and eh-still no gold?"

When I came back to the United States, I told everyone I met the king. People look at you differently when you tell them you've had a king at your show. Every comic has been on Comedy Central and *The Tonight Show*. Not every comic has performed in front of a king. Suddenly it became a credit.

"This next comedian has performed in front of the king of Jordan. Give it up for the king's good friend, Maz Jobrani."

I even got another e-mail from the king's people: "Dear Maz, the king would like your phone number."

The king's staff were masters of vague and curt e-mails. Being the paranoid comedian I am, my mind started racing again. Why did the king want my phone number? Did I say something to offend him? Does he want me to perform at his son's birthday? What if I perform and I bomb? He'll definitely have me killed then. I knew this friendship with the king was going to end badly!

I sent my phone number and got an immediate response: "The king will call you tomorrow."

What? Why does the king want to call me? Is there something we need to discuss? Can't he elaborate in these e-mails?

The next day the phone rang: "The king will call you in five minutes."

It was the countdown to the king. I had no idea what the call was about, but I wanted to make sure no one called me on the other line. I quickly phoned my wife: "Don't call me in the next five minutes. The king of Jordan is calling." Then I hung up on her. I figured this was covering all bases, but mostly I just wanted to brag that I would be having a conversation with a king. When you've been married for a few years sometimes you need a wingman to get your wife excited. What better wingman than the king of Jordan? I was definitely having sex at some point in the future based on this phone call.

For the next four minutes, I just sat and stared at my phone. Finally, it rang: "Please hold for the king of Jordan."

What if he wanted me to become an ambassador? Or perhaps he was going to tell me, like in the olden days, that he was so enamored by my stage antics, he wanted me to follow him around telling jokes all day long, the official Jordanian jester. No sooner was I preparing my responses than a jovial, slightly British voice spoke.

"Hello Maz, how are you?"

"Great, sir. So nice to hear from you."

"How are the boys?"

"They're fine. Busy doing shows. How can I help you?"

"Nothing. Just checking in."

"Just checking in?" I asked. "That's it?"

"Yep, that's it. You take care now."

As soon as he hung up I called my wife, excited.

"The king of Jordan just called to check in with ME!"

"And?"

"That's it!"

"No gold? No cash?"

"You been talking to my mom?"

"I just figured there might be something more, that's all."

"Am I getting laid tonight?"

"Probably not."

Heckled by Jesus

I've traveled to Jordan several times. It's a beautiful country. From Amman to the Dead Sea to Petra, there's so much to see and experience. One of the things I don't enjoy about Jordan, however, is the smoking. It seems like everyone smokes as though he's *trying* to get cancer. In America, we have the right to bear arms; in Jordan, they have the right to puff smokes. Either way, we all have the right to kill ourselves so at least we've got that in common. People in the West think war kills a lot of people in the Middle East, but in reality it's the smoking that does it. Why drop bombs when you can drop Marlboros?

To say that they smoke like chimneys is to not give them enough credit. They smoke more like industrial-waste plants. Maybe part of it has to do with their being surrounded by war all the time and using it to relieve stress. The biggest part of it, I think, is that the antismoking campaign that has occurred in the

West hasn't quite arrived in the Middle East yet. I am so used to smoking not being permitted in restaurants that when I end up in a country where they have smoking sections, I feel like I'm back in the eighties. No offense to smokers, but this whole idea of having a smoking section in any indoor space is the most ridiculous idea ever. It's not like the smoke stops at a certain border and the people in the nonsmoking section don't smell it. It's amazing how cigarette smoke can ruin a perfectly good Jordanian lunch. I think that there should be a rule that if smoking is allowed in a restaurant then you're allowed to go to the smoking section and fart at their tables. Enjoy the baba ghanoush! Smoking is so prevalent that you would think that every Jordanian is issued a carton of cigarettes when he turns fourteen. Chances are they're bootleg cigarettes, but they still stink nonetheless.

Some of the amazing places that we visited included the River Jordan, where John the Baptist allegedly baptized Jesus. As we approached I joked that maybe John didn't take Jesus in the water to baptize him, but rather he took him in there to wash out the cigarette smoke or give him a haircut. What if, in reality, John the Baptist was actually John the Barber? Think about it. It could be true! Why else would he take Jesus, who had long hair, into the water and dip his head in? I say he did it to give him a deep shampoo before giving him a cut.

In the middle of my sacrilegious joking, our tour manager, Candice, who was a practicing Christian, walked into the church that sat by the edge of the river where Jesus had been baptized. She went in to pray, and as she was praying she looked in her palms and saw blood. For an instant she thought it was stigmata, but it turned out to be a bloody nose. Still, that made me stop joking about Jesus. Maybe he really was baptized there and was sending me a sign to stop making fun of him. Yes, I was heckled by Jesus Christ in Jordan.

Indiana Jones and the Temple of Bootleg

Another cool site I visited was Petra, which was recently chosen one of the New Wonders of the World. Petra is truly amazing because it was built thousands of years ago, long before they had the technology that we do. Yet they created these awe-inspiring carvings in stone that run throughout the city. Anyone who goes to Jordan should make the trip to Petra. It will put your life in perspective. That said, be prepared to be peddled tons of Indiana Jones crap, since that's where they shot one of the films. No matter where you go, it's good to know that American capitalism will find you. In the middle of an ancient city built thousands of years ago, surrounded by Bedouins who are indigenous to the region, you will hear them calling, "Indy! Indy! You want buy Indiana Jones hat?" And if you say no, they persist. "Come, my friend. For you I give discount."

Another attraction in Petra were the donkeys and camels you could get on and take pictures with. My whole life I've been running from stereotypes like "towel head" and "camel jockey," and yet, when faced with the opportunity to wrap a keffiyeh around my head and get on a camel, I jumped. I don't know what it is, but when you're a tourist you just act like a tourist. I wonder if that happens to everyone no matter how cool they are? When George Clooney goes to the Leaning Tower of Pisa, does he take a picture where it looks like he's the one holding up the tower? Whatever it was, I couldn't resist. Now I have a picture of me being a towel head and a camel jockey at the same time. If they had offered me a bazooka to hold over one shoulder, I probably would have hoisted that up, too. Come to think of it, I could use some new headshots.

As we left Petra, we noticed a group of young Jordanians walking in the opposite direction holding their skateboards. We passed them and heard, "Maz Jobrani! Persian cat! Meow!" They were quoting my jokes. In the depths of that ancient city, I, Maz Jobrani, had been recognized. My comedy had finally made a mark.

"Did you see me on YouTube?" I asked.

"Nah. Bootleg DVD, one dollar."

Home, Sweet Home

I have two young children, a boy and a girl. Anyone who has children will tell you they are the best things in the world. They're also the most exhausting things. When you have young kids at home, your entire goal, from the moment they wake up, is to make them tired. All day you're saying things like, "Run, run! Climb, climb! Fly! You can fly! Try flapping your arms. You'll fly!" I even purchased a trampoline to accelerate their exhaustion—sort of like playtime steroids for children. I'll sit outside with a cold glass of lemonade watching them bounce, for hours if I have to, whatever it takes to get the job done. "Do a flip! Okay, now do another flip. Now flip your sister. Now flip her while flipping yourself. Now bounce for forty-five minutes while flipping the dog. I know we don't have a dog. Go chase one and bring it back and bounce it on the trampoline while flipping your sister." All the while I'm smiling at how tired this is making them, and how smart I am for thinking of it, so long as no one falls off and breaks an appendage.

No matter how elaborate your scheming, when it comes time to go to bed, kids don't want to sleep. It's like they're allergic to it. They think if they sleep they will be missing some of the fun that's coming when they're conked out. But there's no fun coming. As a parent, you're too exhausted for fun. You've been watching them bounce on the trampoline all day. Watching kids bounce can be an exhausting exercise when you're over forty.

Here's what you have to do if you have babies or are expecting babies at some point: sleep train. Let the little, ungrateful, time-consuming brats cry it out when they're about six months old. You just let them cry and cry in the crib until they cry their bald little heads to sleep. Your wife will want to go in to pick them up and soothe them, but you have to be strong and do anything you can to keep her out. Sing to her, write her some poetry, turn on *Keeping Up with the Kardashians*. Whatever it takes, because after three or four days of crying, the baby will learn to sleep and life goes on. It's a very modern, Western, and cold-blooded method, but it works. Unfortunately, my wife and I come from immigrant backgrounds. Immigrants don't sleep train. Immigrants are all in the bed together. I'm in the bed. My wife's in the bed. The baby's in the bed. My mother-in-law is in the bed. There's a rooster in the bed. My cousins are under the bed. No one is sleeping. And we're all watching the Kardashians!

Always Pack *Ice Age*

I'm not sleeping much anyway. But like most parents, I love my kids, so I try to work my schedule to be around them as much as possible. Sometimes that means taking them on the road with me. We first did this when my wife and I only had our son and I had a one-month tour in the Middle East. At the time he was a year and a half and we quickly learned a great lesson—*Ice Age* can be your best friend. Or better said, any animation can calm your kid down, get him quiet, and stop the other passengers from giving you the dirty looks they've been issuing you since the plane took off and your kid began screaming. When this would happen, I would usually hand the kid off to my wife and start smiling at the other passengers: "Yeah, his mother really hasn't done a good job with him. If we had moved to Iran when he was born like I suggested, he would be much better behaved. Because in Iran, if you cry on a plane they cut off your hands. It's true. I heard it on Fox News."

That was our first trip, with our first kid. We had no idea what we were doing. We packed the stuff we thought we needed—milk, diapers, toys, whiskey (just in case the kid needed to be drugged), extra whiskey (just in case that didn't work and *we* needed to be drugged). Halfway through our flight, my son was getting restless and had to be walked. This is something kids do, walk up and down the aisle for hours, with no destination, just seeing what everyone else is doing. You would think they're training for a marathon—some little toddler marathon where they walk for 26.2 miles, just waddling along and taking milk breaks, but no pee breaks because they're racing in diapers. (By the way, if any marathoner is reading this now, that's not a bad idea. Next time you're in a race try wearing a diaper and see how much that cuts off your time. You're welcome.)

As I walked him up and down the aisle, acting like his personal trainer, the boy caught a glimpse of *Ice Age* on someone's screen. He froze. It was a magical moment because I had been pleading with him for an hour to relax and take a seat. I had tried every ploy and then, bam! It happened. He saw the cartoon and he gave up on his ambition to set the world walking record at thirty thousand feet.

Soon after that flight, we purchased every video viewing device we could get our hands on. First it was a video player with a headset. Then it was an iPad where we downloaded a ton of programs. Then it was an iPod, which had the same programs but on a smaller screen. Every time our son would act up on a plane, we would queue up *Ice Age*, shove a device at his face, and he would be hypnotized. We even bought an old DVD of Tom and Jerry in Dubai, most likely a bootleg. The combined efforts of that cat and mouse beating the shit out of each other with pots and pans got us through our one-month journey across the Middle East. I don't know if I will regret this one day when he comes home from school and they tell me he banged someone over the head with a frying pan, but for those few weeks traveling was magical.

The Minibar, My Wingman

Traveling with kids has its own set of challenges. A friend gave me sound advice when she said that you should book the flight for their sleep time and make sure you don't have any layovers. Just make it as streamlined as possible. It's like you're a Navy SEAL team and you need to get them from point A to B in the most sedated state possible.

And getting them there is only half the battle. When you're traveling without kids, you get into a city and ask the concierge if there are any plays you should see, or if there are any restaurants you should visit, or, if it happens to be your thing, is there a specific park you should go to in order to score some weed, hash, heroin, crack, ice cream, etc. Sometimes you just check into the hotel, go upstairs, and take a nap. Who knows, maybe you watch TV. CNN? Sure. ESPN? Why not? Adult channels? Hey, you only live once.

When you're traveling with kids, it's a whole different experience. Arriving in the hotel, you spend the first thirty minutes dragging the kid away from the fountain they've put in the middle of the lobby. Why do hotels feel like they need a fountain in the lobby? Do they think the guests checking in will want to go for a quick swim? Is it the soothing sound that's supposed to distract you from the fact that you're in a concrete building in a chain hotel in some bustling city that's anything but soothing? A toddler during check-in turns you into a lifeguard, the lobby warden, and a grief counselor, all at once. "Come here. Here! Let's go. Come on. Yes, that's water. Yes, fishy. You want to throw a coin in there? Here's a coin. Ow! Don't throw it AT Daddy! No, Daddy's not angry. Stop crying! STOP CRYING, GODDAMMIT! Sorry, Daddy didn't mean to cuss. No, don't tell Mommy! Here, watch *Ice Age!*"

When you travel with a toddler, the first thing you do in the hotel room is empty the minibar because your kid will insist on opening it and fondling all the items. You place the mini bottles of whiskey, vodka, and tequila on the top shelf in the closet in hopes that you will return it at the end of your trip. But you're only fooling yourself because after a full day of wrestling with the kid, you will see those bottles just sitting there speaking to you: "Drink me! You know you need me. Just a taste won't hurt. Open me up and drink me with your wife. If you get her drunk enough she may actually have sex with you. I can be your wingman. I know I'm overpriced, but the kid's asleep. Anything is possible! You deserve a little luxury."

The concierge at a hotel is your best friend—the third parent in this deal, really. This is a person who is in it with you—he wants to help because, like you, he wants to tire the kid out so he or she sleeps instead of irritating other guests and swimming in the fountain. Does the hotel have activities? Is there a pool? Is there a kids' space where you can take the kid and run him around? You're exhausted from your twenty-hour flight into a completely different time zone, but you can't just tell the kid to chill. He won't do it. He's on Los Angeles time, and even though it's 9:00 p.m. in Dubai, it's only 9:00 a.m. in Los Angeles. He's just waking up! So you take the kid down to the lobby and have him play with the fountain again because the pool and the kids' space are closed. Besides, the kids' space will cost you fifty bucks for a half hour, and it's just a room with a few books, some videos, and enough phlegmy viruses to cause an influenza outbreak in most American cities.

Soon the time difference, a near-fountain-drowning, and subsequent sea rescue by you have the expected effect and the kid runs out of energy. Then you put him in bed with a mountain of pillows around him so he won't roll out and onto the floor, and eventually out of the hotel room, which is totally possible because you're about to get pretty damn drunk. Now it's party time. You and your wife get situated in the TV area (yes, you have to get a suite when you have a kid), and you quickly realize that the baby will be getting up in a few hours, which means you have to down those miniature bottles pronto! You drink, you flirt, you stretch. Looks like the sex is finally going to happen. You go to the bathroom to freshen up, and by the time you return, you look over and you've managed to put your wife to sleep with all the booze you've given her in such a short time. You glare at that tequila bottle and think, *What happened to the sex? What kind of wingman are you? You lied to me.*

The next day, you wake up exhausted and take your kid to the hotel fountain for his morning exercise, only to learn he's now tired of that activity. So you consult with your old friend, the concierge, about local parks or children's museums. In Amman we took him to the king's car museum, where a collection of cars the king and his father had accumulated were on display. This also included the task of keeping him behind the velvet ropes and not touching the cars. Velvet ropes are meant to keep kids away from pricey items, but they have the opposite effect. Kids see these ropes and think it would be fun to go under them and around them and over them. Instead of looking at it nicely, they eventually fall into the pricey item that the rope was supposed to protect and break it. It's a disaster!

In Beirut, my wife took our son to the kids' play area to give me time to nap. I hadn't noticed, but most of the nannies in Lebanon were Indian, and so is my wife. Just as I was settling in, she came barging back into the room.

"I'm appalled!" she shouted.

"What happened?"

"They thought I was his nanny."

"Why would they think that?"

"Because all the nannies are Indian."

I needed to sleep. And in order to do that, I needed to get in front of this situation. "I know. I'm appalled, too," I replied. "You go back and let them know that he's your son. I'll stay here in bed thinking of a long letter we can write the Lebanese government as soon as I'm up from my nap."

"I'm not going back."

"If you don't go back I'll be forced to call the hotel management and let them know my nanny is acting up!"

That joke didn't go over too well. A few minutes later I found myself in the kids' play area with my son and the Indian nannies while my wife was upstairs napping.

Dead Horse, Wet Tears

One of my best feelings is when I'm returning from a trip and my plane is hovering above Los Angeles. I've traveled the world and there really isn't any other place that has the L.A. weather. No matter where I'm coming from, chances are the weather I'm flying home to is nicer. The bigger excitement comes in knowing I will be seeing my family soon. Having children is like being Fred Flintstone and coming home to Dino the dinosaur. They rush to see you and hug you and hold your hand. You're their hero and those first moments back are magical. Of course, ask any parent and they'll tell you this feeling fades when that same night they start getting tired, having meltdowns, and screaming in your ear. Quickly you go from being happy to be home to screaming at them to go to bed. Someone once said, "If you're not yelling at your kids then you're not spending enough time with them." At that point you start planning your next trip away from the little runts.

My kids have managed to make me more sensitive. Before my children were born, I didn't get emotional that often. But ever since they came into my life, things have changed. When my son was an infant, I started getting teary eyed watching commercials. There was one Tide commercial where a dad was drying his son with a towel and I remember thinking how beautiful it was. The next thing I knew I was tearing up. Soon I wasn't just crying about being a father, but also about becoming such a pussy, and contemplating when all this nonsense began, and how pissed off my wife would be if she caught me crying during Tide commercials. We don't even use Tide!

It wasn't just the one time either. Another time I was watching an HBO show called *Luck* on an airplane where a horse had fallen in a race and had to be put to sleep. They showed a close-up of the horse's eye as it lay on the ground. I'm not an animal person, but I found myself inexplicably weeping. Crying on an airplane is extra awkward because you're surrounded by people and you try to hide it by continuing to look straight ahead as you weep. That works until you begin sniffling and then the people around you start giving you weird looks, so you have to point at the screen to show them the dying horse.

"They're putting him to sleep. Can you believe it?"

"It's a TV show. Get ahold of yourself."

"I don't know who's playing the part of the horse," you mutter, trying to save face as you wipe away snot, a giant, man-sized booger. "But they're doing a really great job. Must be Daniel Day-Lewis. Totally believable."

Double Baby Duty

When I was a child, my dad taught me that men don't cry, but growing up in Iran we didn't have laundry detergent commercials with such exceptional acting. Once I had my own kids, they taught me that it's okay to cry, just not on airplanes. These two worlds came together when my dad came to Los Angeles to spend the last few months of his life with us. He had been living in Tehran and had been sick. Toward the end of his life he was on all kinds of medications: Xanax, Percocet, Ambien, you name it. He was a pharmaceutical company's wet dream. I don't know if it's an Iranian thing, but every older Iranian I know seems to be on a bunch of medications at the same time. I don't think they go to the doctor. They just meet at parties and prescribe medications to one another. Everyone has a doctor in the family, so getting the prescriptions filled is easy. No one monitors if the drugs are safe to take together. They just take them, zone out, and relay the wonders of modern pharmaceuticals at the next gathering. I'm guessing that teenagers do this same sort of thing, but with ecstasy, cocaine, and other mood-enhancing drugs. The old folks take stuff to slow them down, and the young folks take stuff to speed them up. Same idea, just fifty years apart.

When my dad came to stay with us, he wasn't in good shape. It was sad watching illness consume a man who had been such a lion in life. He was the one who taught me that anything is possible and to never sweat the small stuff. My dad had always given me the feeling that you can take on the world and win. I get a lot of my confidence from him. But there he was, at seventy-six, unable to beat time. All those years of living hard caught up to him. He liked to say he was seventy-six but had lived the life of a seven-hundred-year-old.

It was important for me to have my dad meet my son even in the state he was in. My son was an infant when my father arrived in Los Angeles. Quickly I was reminded of how things were done old school versus how they are done today. At one point the baby was crying and my dad needed a glass of water.

"Son, can you pelease get me a glass of vater?"

"Give me a second, Dad, I have to soothe the baby. He's crying."

"He is a baby. Dat's vhat babies do. Dey cry."

"I know that, Dad, but I need to rock him."

"Rock him? You vant him to be a man or a pussy?"

"He's a baby!"

"And I am your fadder. Get me deh vater."

"Dad, chill! Here, have another Xanax."

"Tank you. Now, I need some vater to take it."

It was like having two babies in the house.

My father had been in the hospital because of complications from an operation he had to remove a benign tumor above his eye. Once the tumor was removed, there was a space in his brain that eventually caused seizures. It was one of the toughest things in my life to watch my father have seizures in front of my eyes and not be able to do anything about it. I remember New Year's Eve 2008 going out to celebrate with my wife and then having to go to the hospital to spend the night with my dad, who had been put into a coma to stop the seizures. We had hopes that he would make a comeback, but that was not to be.

He hung in there until March 2009, when we got a call from the hospital telling us that he'd had a stroke. I will never forget the nurse who was so good to us at the hospital. When you are going through something like that, once in a while you have an angel come into your life. For my family, that angel was our male nurse Colin. He was very sensitive and caring to my dad and he called my sister the day my dad had the stroke to let her know. He told her they could resuscitate him but that he would not make a good recovery and it could just extend his misery. My sister asked what Colin would do if it were his own father and he said, "I would let him go with some dignity."

I was due to fly to Rutgers University for a show the next day and then on to Houston for shows that weekend. I was in the hospital room with my sister, aunt, cousin, and wife trying to decide if I should cancel the shows. That's the difficulty of having a job in which you really can't call in sick. There's not someone who can do your job if you're the headliner and don't arrive. I felt extra bad because the kids at Rutgers who had organized the show had been in touch with me for over a year and they said they were really looking forward to finally having me out. I felt obligated to make the shows, but we really didn't know how long it would take my father to pass. It could be a few weeks, so there was a chance that I could go do the shows and come back in time to be next to him when he passed.

I decided around two in the morning that I should go home and pack so that I could make my flight at eight. I felt that that was what my father would want me to do—handle my business. As I was walking to the parking lot with my wife, she reminded me that if I went to New Jersey and my father passed while I was gone I would never forgive myself. Furthermore, she made the good point that I would have a tough time performing if I got there and found out that my father had died. Right then I knew there was a reason why I had married a lawyer. She knew how to make an argument and seal the deal.

Fortunately, I listened. The next morning, when I would have been on a plane to the East Coast, my father passed away while I was in the room seated next to him. I was happy to have stayed by his side. His passing occurred only nine months after my son's birth. It was as if my son came into my life to replace that relationship. Dhara was too young to know what was happening, but we dressed him in a white Indian outfit for the funeral and took him with us. His jolly little face helped me get through what felt like a long day of Tide commercials and dead horses.

My father's funeral was the second funeral I had been to for a close relative. The one before had been in 2003 for my grandfather, who also had been a great influence in my life. He was the one who taught me to never live your life saying "what if." He would say the word "if" is a bad word. It is a word that takes you away from your reality. The way he put it was, "Never say what if I had done this or what if I had done that. You've got to live with what you decide to do because that is your reality. For example, if my aunt had a penis she would be my uncle. End of story!" I told you he was a poet.

With my father, I had my son to lean on to get me through, while with my grandfather I leaned on my family. There was also an alcoholic lady who lived in our building when my grandfather passed away who tried to console me. Here is some advice: If you are drunk, don't try to console anyone who's grieving. This lady came over to our apartment the night my grandfather passed, looked up at the sky, and issued some tender words.

"Don't worry, Maz. Your grandfather hasn't left us. He's with us. His spirit is with us."

"Thank you. I appreciate the kind words."

"No, really, look up in the sky. You see that star? That's your grandfather."

I looked up and noticed the star was moving. She stared at it, and then we both stared at it until she finally took a sip of her drink.

"No, wait," she corrected herself. "That's not a star. That's an airplane. Your grandfather is definitely not on that plane. But trust me, he's with us."

Santa Might Be Muslim

People often ask me if my wife is religious. It usually means that the person asking is religious and they want to know if we're raising our kids Muslim or Hindu. I think to them it's like a football game, and they want to know who won. They're often taken aback when I tell them that neither of us is really religious and that I was born in a Muslim family while she was born in a Christian family. When I say that my family was Muslim, it just means that we lived in Iran, which is a Shiite Muslim country. My parents never prayed or fasted or made a trip to Mecca. The closest thing we had to a religious person in my family was my grandmother, who thought she was religious but really was just superstitious.

"Vhen you go to a casino," Grandma would preach, "say a prayer to Allah and den put all your money on be-lack. You are guaranteed to vin."

"Grandma, isn't gambling a sin?"

"Only if you lose."

My grandmother also taught me to appreciate what I have in her own religious/superstitious way. When I was five years old in Iran, she told me that whenever I saw anyone who was less fortunate that I should look up in the sky and say a prayer where I thank Allah seven times. It was the equivalent of saying seven Hail Marys and thanking God. This became a full-time job, since living in a busy city like Tehran you saw a lot of misery and poverty. I would be in the backseat of my mother's car and see someone in a wheelchair. I would look to the sky and start thanking Allah seven times. By the time I was at my sixth thanks, I would see a homeless person slouched in a doorway and start thanking Allah again. Next I would see a midget then a blind person then an albino. I wasn't even sure if albinos counted, but I would thank Allah for not making me one anyway. Pretty soon, my trips into downtown Tehran with my mom and grandmother became full-on sermons. To this day, whenever I see someone less fortunate than me, I thank God, but only once, and a nonspecific god. Such are the ways of a busy Muslim-ish person in the twenty-first century.

I'm the only person in my immediate family who has actually visited Mecca. I did this on a trip to Saudi Arabia where I was doing a show in Jeddah. I asked the locals how far away Mecca was, and they told me about forty-five minutes. I was tired from my flight and wanted to nap, but I was not about to get that close to Mecca and not see it. Not because I was religious, but out of curiosity. Also because I knew that when I told people I had been to Saudi Arabia, someone would ask, "Did you go to Mecca?"

It would be like going to Anaheim and not seeing Disneyland, or going to the Vatican and not seeing the Sistine Chapel, which almost happened to me as well. This was when I was on a junior year abroad program in college. I was never a museum type, so I would get bored listening to the docent go on and on about a painting or sculpture. When I was in Rome, I decided to go off on my own to see the Vatican and made a point to see the Sistine Chapel. (Not because I wanted to, but because I knew that when I told people I had been to Rome, someone would ask, "Did you see the Sistine Chapel?" It seems like throughout my life I've experienced a lot of things just so I can tell people I have done them. You can say I like to please.) The problem with my trip to the Vatican was that I wasn't 100 percent sure what the Sistine Chapel looked like, or what it was, and I didn't go with a tour guide. All I knew was that it had been painted by either Michelangelo or Leonardo or one of the other Teenage Mutant Ninja Turtles. I wasn't sure which one. Anyone who's been there will tell you that the Vatican is a really big place, and I was on a deadline because I had to meet someone for lunch. At that age, lunch was the priority.

As I walked in and out of rooms, I tried to listen in on the docents taking other people around on tours to see if one would say something like, "And now, please turn your eyes upon the Sistine

Chapel." I never heard those words. When I finally found myself in a small room with a cool painting on the ceiling, I figured this must be it. I looked around and there weren't that many people in the room, which I found odd. I would have thought that there would be crowds of people observing it, sketching it, posing for pictures with it, but nothing. I looked up for about ten seconds and tried to act like I knew what the hell I was doing. I put my hand to my chin and fake pondered this classic's relevance to my life. In reality I was just counting backward from ten so that I could make it seem like I had spent enough time appreciating what I thought was the Sistine Chapel in case someone was watching. Then I took off and started following the exit signs out of the place. It wasn't until a few minutes into my exit route when I walked into a huge room where I saw people looking up and camping out, observing the art above in awe. I recognized the famous touching fingers that Michelangelo had painted. Oh shit, THIS was the Sistine Chapel? How stupid of me to have thought it was the other room. This was the real deal! Once again I put my hand to my chin and started pondering the magic of this historical piece of art. In reality I was just counting backward: "Ten, nine, eight, seven . . ."

So I've been to the Vatican and I've been to Mecca—not because I wanted to, but just so I could tell you that I've been to the Vatican and Mecca. I hope you appreciate what I've done for you. I've also been to many bar mitzvahs and eaten matzo balls at my friend's Shabbat dinners. All these experiences have had some spiritual effects on me, but I still don't consider myself religious. I would say the closest religious belief I have is Zoroastrianism, which was the first monotheistic religion. Their tenets are "Good words, good thoughts, good deeds." As long as you live by that then you send a positive energy into the world. Live and let live.

Epilogue

Now that I have written this book, I realize that a lot of my issues have been created in my own head. Like I said at the start, writing a book is like doing therapy, and I feel like I've made really good breakthroughs. First of all, I can say without a doubt that I am not a terrorist. I mean, I knew that from the start, but given what the media and movies have been saying about people who look like me over the past thirty years, I was beginning to question myself. If I wasn't a terrorist, why was I playing so many of them on TV? Why was I feeling guilty going through airports? Why was I so good at ululating at weddings?

Furthermore, what I've learned from reflecting on my travels and writing this book is that most people are inherently good. However, there are also people who just don't get it. They are out to hate and judge you just because of the label that you fit. There are those who will think that just because I'm of Middle Eastern descent that means that I have it in for America and am just waiting for the right opportunity to open up a can of jihad on this country. They won't look at the fact that the majority of Middle Easterners and Muslims really don't hate America as much as Fox News would have you believe. And technically, I'm not even that Middle Eastern, given that I grew up in the United States. If anything, I'm Middle Eastern light. I swear, look at my picture on the cover of this book. I'm not even that hairy! I'm bald, but even worse, I've got receding eyebrows. How the hell do you get receding eyebrows?

I knew I was Middle Eastern light after September 11 when the airport profiling never happened. The only person profiling me turned out to be me! After a while, I started to get offended that they weren't stopping me. I felt like running through the airport just randomly screaming Middle Eastern and Muslim names in hopes they would stop and search me: "MOHAMMAD, ABDULLAH, RAHIM!" But I'm sure that my receding eyebrows would have kept me out of trouble. "You can't be a terrorist. Look at your eyebrows. Come on through, buddy."

I've come to live my life with this philosophy: Chances are that at some point you will either get hit by a tree or eaten by a bear. I haven't done the scientific research to prove this, but I know that something random will happen at some point in my life. This happened to me between the time I wrote this book and the time I edited it: One Tuesday I awoke to several messages left on my phone by my mother. You know something bad has happened when you see three messages from your mom at seven in the morning. When I called her back she gave me the bad news. My brother Kashi had died.

This was a shock to my family and me and it hit us all very hard. I rushed to my mom's house, where he lived with his seven-year-old son, and found him passed away. This was the hardest thing I had ever experienced in my life, and as we sat in my mother's living room discussing the funeral options I decided to repeat what I had done so much of in my life: travel. I had shows to do in Chicago that weekend; I figured I should stick to my work, since there wasn't much else for me to do. I told my friends I had read once that Brett Favre played in a football game when his father died, and that my brother would have wanted me to stick to my schedule and do the shows.

As I got closer to Thursday, when I would be traveling, I began to have my doubts. Still, I got on a plane from Los Angeles and flew to Chicago. It wasn't until I landed on the tarmac in Chicago at noon on the day of a show that it hit me: How the hell was I going to be funny when my brother had just died? Why was I running, and what was I running from? I guess it was a coping mechanism, trying to convince myself that life goes on and not allowing myself to mourn. I got off the plane, called my manager and asked him to get me out of the gigs. I was coming home. That weekend I was able to be home with my family and I was so happy to be there and mourn and hug and cry and give myself a chance to feel the pain. In the weeks that followed, I leaned on the love of friends, family, and strangers to get me through this hard time, and I also was surprised to see how many other people had lost loved ones unexpectedly. My wife sent me an article claiming that a twenty-second hug has healing qualities, and so I went around hugging people for as long as I could. It took a tragedy like this to remind me how much love is in the world and how petty we can become if we forget it.

So I say to you people who are reading this book, be nice to one another. Why hate someone simply because he has a different belief or different skin color? It's amazing how far out of their way people will go to differentiate themselves from their enemies, when the reality is that we have so much in common. For example, did you know that both Jews and Palestinians eat falafel? Did you know that both Muslims and Christians believe in Jesus? Did you know that Iranians, like Americans, enjoy pizza? If we could stop fighting one another because of color and race and religion, and concentrate on who the real enemies are . . . our children! If we could just get them to go to sleep!

What I'm saying is if we could all concentrate on the things we have in common and celebrate those things together, then we might succeed in making the world a better place and looking up, so that the next time a tree is about to fall on us we could zigzag and survive. Only to later be eaten by a bear.

Acknowledgments

I would like to begin by thanking the three essential people who made this book possible: Jesus Christ, Elvis Presley, and, of course, Justin Bieber.

Gotcha.

I always read the acknowledgments section of books, looking for famous people's names so I can see if the author has any big-shot friends. I actually don't know any of those people, but now I've got some famous names in my acknowledgments, and anyone thinking of just skimming this section might as well read the entire thing at this point.

Now, for the people whom I actually know and want to thank, let me begin with my manager and business partner, Ray Moheet, who encouraged me to write this book. He has always championed me and been the best partner to have in this world of acting and stand-up. Thank you, Ray, for pushing me to succeed. By the way, if you have any problems with what I've written, please e-mail Ray because it's all his fault. I also want to thank my agent, David Patterson, who is the most light-skinned Latino I know. David, thank you for being smart, competent, and professional. And thank you even more for getting this book sold. Thanks to Jon Methven, who helped in writing this book. Jon was my sounding board and partner throughout. He acted as my editor before we actually got the book to my editor. Speaking of editors, thanks to Sarah Knight, who took a chance on me. I'd say she's smart just for doing that, but she also went to Harvard, so she's been smart since long before she met me. Because of her I can now call myself an author. (Not sure how good an author, but an author nonetheless.) Thanks to photographer Paul Mobley for taking my cover pictures and making me look goofily unthreatening. Thanks to Mitzi Shore for making me a regular at the Comedy Store and giving me a place to grow as a comedian. Thanks to Jamie Masada for giving me a second home at the Laugh Factory and filling me with wine and love every time I'm there. I love you, buddy! Thanks to Candice Ortiz, Robin Tate, Heidi Feigin, Ali Benmohamed, Josh Katz, Judi Brown, Norman Aladjem, Robert Hartman, Tim Scally, Mitchell K. Stubbs, and Judi Page. Thanks to all my friends and family who have been in my life and given me so much love. If I forget to mention you by name here, I'm sorry. Thanks to my aunts Roxanna, Mandana, and Mahin. Thanks to my cousins Amir, Ali, Shahriar, Mahmoud, Majid, Shiva, Shaheen, Mahtab, Alex, and Salar.

Thanks to my mom, who really isn't as mean as I make her out to be in this book. She's actually a very elegant and sweet woman, and if I could have withstood all those hours of reading fine print and contracts, I would have become a lawyer just to make her happy. Mom, I love you! Thanks to my grandmother for teaching me how to appreciate what I have. Thanks to my sister, Mariam, for being my other half in life. Thanks to my other sister, Kiana, for coming into my life when I was a young adult and bringing even more love to me. Thanks to my brother Kashi for reminding me to slow down and spend time with the ones I love. I miss you, man! Thanks to my other brother, Joey, for always being there when I need you. Thanks to my nephew, Kamran, for being a wise soul who we all love. Thanks to my kids, Dhara and Mila, for making me love deeper than I've ever loved before. And last, but not least, thanks to my wife, Pretha, for being my partner on this ride and for putting up with my silly jokes and long absences from home. You're the most beautiful woman I've ever known and you get more beautiful every day. I love you, baby!

In loving memory of my younger brother, Kashi Jobrani.

About the Author

MAZ JOBRANI was born in Iran but grew up in America, which means he has a blue passport so he's okay. He was a founding member of the Axis of Evil Comedy Tour, which was a stand-up tour that premiered on Comedy Central and performed in front of the king of Jordan. So basically, he's better than you. Maz has had two solo Showtime comedy specials and continues to tour internationally. In film, Maz appeared in *Friday after Next*, *The Interpreter*, and *13 Going On 30*. On TV, he's appeared in ABC's *Better Off Ted*, HBO's *Curb Your Enthusiasm* and Showtime's *Shameless*. He is a regular panelist on NPR's "Wait Wait . . . Don't Tell Me!" and has given two TED Talks. It's a good thing he has no hair or it would've all fallen out from all the traveling he does. He's got Executive Platinum status on American Airlines, which means he gets free sandwiches when he flies.